# God Is Close to the Brokenhearted

## Good News for Those Who Are Depressed

Rachel Callahan, C.S.C., and
Rea McDonnell, S.S.N.D.

## ST. ANTHONY MESSENGER PRESS

Cincinnati, Ohio

In gratitude to our parents,

*LILL & ED CALLAHAN*

and

*MARIE & JOHN MCDONNELL*

# Contents

# Introduction

It is winter as we write. The winter light is different: softer, yet paradoxically harsh. Even in this muted light, however, we can see farther because the leaves have fallen from the trees. These dark days challenge us to trust that beneath the barrenness and death lies a promise of life and light.

We write for those who suffer depression and who, from its depths, seek peace, healing and God's own self. The two parts of the book are structured around these words from the Psalms:

> Our God is close to the brokenhearted.
> Those who are crushed in Spirit God saves.
> *(Psalm 34:19)*

In Part One we describe various kinds of depression that afflict the brokenhearted. We intersperse images of the experience of depression with basic information. We also investigate some images of God that may need to be reexamined during times of depression.

In Part Two we explore God's healing, saving action. Our suggestions for prayer and reflection are based on Scripture, bodily senses, memory and imagination. Because depression springs from, lives in and torments the whole person, our healing will be deeper if we bring more of ourselves before God.

Our credentials for writing about depression and spirituality include Rachel Callahan's Ph.D. in clinical psychology and Rea McDonnell's Ph.D. in biblical studies. Over the past twenty-five years each of us has listened to the brokenhearted, Rachel as a therapist and Rea as a teacher, spiritual director and pastoral counselor. We have also both been depressed ourselves at various times in our lives. Rachel's depression tends to slow her down; Rea's tends to be an agitated depression. From our own experience we know that our true healer is God.

Many friends, family and community members, therapists and spiritual directors through the years have guided us or supported us in our own inner journeys, putting flesh on God for us. Thanks especially to Shaun McCarty, S.T.; Bob Doherty, S.J.; Mary Irving, S.S.N.D.; Olivia Marie Hutcheson, C.S.C.; Kathy McNany, O.S.B.; and the late Bob Bolanos, S.J. We write this book in gratitude for our continual healing, a lifelong process of growing in wisdom and grace.

We write with some assumptions. We assume that the resources of a healthy, or healing, spiritual life can amplify the healing methods of the medical and psychological disciplines. We assume, as Carl Jung once noted, that intertwined with any emotional problem is a spiritual crisis. The Greek word *krisis* means "decision time." Yet a lessening ability to make decisions is precisely one of depression's symptoms. "How miserable I am! Who shall save me from this body of death?" Saint Paul cries in anguish (Romans 7:24). "Only God through Christ Jesus," he responds (Romans 7:25).

We write, then, for Christians. We write especially for those who may have assimilated some bad news about God. The good news, repeated in so many ways throughout this book, is that when our feeling is flat, our thinking off-kilter, our concentration weak, our decisionmaking power nil, God "is close to the brokenhearted. Those who are crushed in spirit God saves" (Psalm 34:18).

We believe that God came closest in the person of Jesus, risen and alive now. The risen Lord continues to minister, heal and act on our behalf. We flesh out some Gospel stories, using active imagination. Saint Ignatius of Loyola named this method of being with Christ "contemplation," a way to enter wholeheartedly into the gospel mystery.

The movement from brokenhearted to wholehearted is

God's passionate desire for us. We invite you to cooperate with God's healing by working through the exercises for prayer and reflection interspersed with the blocks of information. Use your bodies, senses, memories, imaginations, minds and wills as helps for healing.

As we embarked upon writing this book we invited friends, colleagues, clients and directees to share their images of depression. Depression is both multifaceted and uniquely personal. We are so grateful to them all for their images and stories.

We are grateful to the editorial staff at St. Anthony Messenger Press; to Katie Mindling, R.S.M., who generously instructed us in computers and frequently rescued us and the manuscript; to the Sisters of the Holy Cross at whose house in Ocean City, Maryland, we did the bulk of our writing; and to our neighbors there, John and Maggie Stasiak. Most especially, thanks be to our God, for putting a new song in our mouths:

> Your kindness and your faithfulness
> We will always proclaim
> In the vast assembly of your faithful ones!
> *(Psalm 40:11)*

# PART ONE

# Longing for God's Peace

*I have waited, waited for the Lord;*
  *God leaned toward me and heard my cry....*
*God drew me out of the pit of destruction.* (Psalm 40:1, 3)

In our Scriptures, the Book of Genesis opens with the Spirit of God, the breath of God, hovering over the abyss, over the waters of chaos. When the creative Spirit breathed life into chaos, creation began. God saw that it was very good. In this book we call on the breath of God to penetrate all that is chaotic deep within us, the abyss of our depression. We have punctuated this book with pauses for reflection and prayer, even—perhaps especially—from "the pit of destruction" (Psalm 40:3). We will pause frequently to long for God's peace.

## For Reflection and Prayer

*Take some deep breaths. Focus your attention on your own breathing. God breathes, you breathe. As you breathe out, let go of your worries. As you breathe in, invite the Spirit to move over whatever troubled waters may be disturbing your heart. Breathe deeply; breathe in the Holy Spirit, whom Scripture calls the breath of God.*

*Ask God to bend down to you and hear you. Invite our God, however you name God, to be with you as you read this book and pray the exercises, as your pain heals. In whatever way(s) you experience and name your brokenness, ask for grace to trust God's desire to heal all that is broken and crushed in you.*

*Our God is close to the brokenhearted. Those who are crushed in spirit, God saves (Psalm 34:18).*

*We suggest that you take time to work with these exercises for reflection and prayer as they are presented. If you jot down some of your thoughts and feelings in a journal after the exercise, you can return to these reflections on your experience. A simple notebook, even a lined yellow legal pad, can offer us a place to sort out our jumbled thoughts and to write the secrets of our hearts. When we read God's sacred Scriptures or read again the holy scripture of our own life experience, that reading makes God's action and our experience present again. When we remember God's grace we let it penetrate our lives once again.*

*When we feel brokenhearted or crushed in spirit, it is helpful to create a safe space where no one or nothing can harm us. We have found it helpful to make a physical space of peace and safety—a room, the corner of a room or a shady place outside. Indoors we might decorate our space with color or pictures. We might bring light into the space with a special candle or lamp. We might use fragrance to create a healing aroma. Photographs of the people, both living and dead, who accept us and love us, who make up our own personal prayer circle, can enhance the peace of this place. Fixing this outside space helps us bring order to the space in our minds. Then, even when we are not physically there, we carry its image and its tranquility throughout our day.*

## Waiting

Depression is a time of burdensome waiting. The oppressive early morning hours, as we lie wakeful in the dark, can seem an eternal now. We lose any sense of a meaningful past or a hopeful future. We remain gripped in hopeless, helpless waiting; one of our respondents names it "an eternal state of static."

It helps at times like this to recall the essential waiting involved in so many life processes. Shortening the waiting time of pregnancy is life-threatening. Winter—cold, dark and bleak—is waiting time for seeds and bulbs, for dead-looking branches that hide the promise of life. When the warmth of a false spring coaxes fragile shoots and tiny stalks of green, they are at risk. Nikos Kazantzakis, in *Zorba the Greek*, tells of a cocoon hurriedly warmed in a human hand; the butterfly within, not having strengthened its new wings in its struggle to emerge, is deformed, disabled and soon dies.

Depression sets before us life and death. Depression's waiting time can bring disablement and death or it can create the struggle that will lead to spring. Albert Camus, in *Summer* (Gallimard, 1954) expressed it this way: "In the depth of winter, I finally learned that within me lay an invincible summer."

## Brokenness

Brokenness is an integral part of the human experience. Brokenness can sap our interior vitality. This book will focus on a particular kind of brokenness, the heartbreak of depression. Whether its source is our inherited biochemistry or events in our lives, depression is a universal human experience and its verbal expression is as old as the written word. In this book we will recall words both from the Jewish and Christian Scriptures and from the holy texts of ordinary people who responded to our call for personal testimonies to the pain of depression.

As we wait in the winter and the dark, in the pain and the pit, aware of our brokenheartedness and longing for God's peace, let us pray together with everyone through the centuries who has ever prayed:

I have waited, waited for the Lord;
God leaned toward me and heard my cry....
God drew me out of the pit of destruction.
*(Psalm 40:1, 3)*

### *For Reflection and Prayer*

*Take some time to journal about your own experience of brokenness. What has "the pit of destruction" been like for you? Be as concrete as possible in naming and claiming your experience. Your pit may involve painful, broken relationships with family or friends. It may be loss or loneliness. It may be sickness or worry. Whatever the contour of the hole in your heart, try to write about it, draw it, mold it in clay or sand or even snow.*

*Then, if you are able, hold this broken heart, with its gouged-out holes, in open hands before your God. This may be painful. Ask the Spirit to teach you. The Spirit will not overwhelm you with the truth of your pain, past or present. If your anxiety rises too quickly, retreat to your safe space, rest and try again another day. There is no need to rush into healing. God knows how to wait.*

## Crushed in Spirit

As we reflect on the experience of depression, we will examine our attitudes and feelings toward it. We feel crushed and our spirits suffer. But beyond that, how do we name our depression? What have we been taught about depression? By whom? How have we learned to deal with it?

Many of us have received subtle and not-so-subtle clues that depression is a character flaw. It is not socially acceptable to show a less than smiling face in public. Expressions of what were once called "negative" emotions—anger, hurt, fear, sadness—were unseemly, even within the privacy of the family. For example, a whimpering or sobbing child was often told: "Stop crying or I'll give you something to cry about." We may have been trained to cut off these emotions from conscious experience; instead of owning and expressing them in healthy ways, we find that they whirl around inside us, trapped in a psychic spin cycle. Such inner chaos robs us of energy and life.

When we are gripped by depression, we may feel the added burden and guilt of not being able to pull out of it. Our families, religious authority figures or even we ourselves may have named our profound loss of hope, felt lack of faith and feelings of despair as moral failing, as sin. The thin-skinned irritability that often accompanies depression may likewise have been termed sin. Lack of energy and inability to concentrate, two symptoms of depression, may have been mislabeled as sloth or just plain laziness. These negative moral tags only enhance our misery because of the shame we feel or are made to feel.

Because depression can manifest itself in physical symptoms, we can spend much time and money seeking elusive cures for *real* pain that has no organic basis. The pain *is* real; we are not crazy. Fortunately the past decade has witnessed a massive effort to educate physicians as well as the general public about some of the very real pain of depression. A national day for screening for depression has raised public awareness that depression is an illness that can be treated.

Depression invades our bodies, and our spirits feel ground down as well. A physician's or friend's suggestion of depression need not be an embarrassment or insult. If we have been taught that expressions of sadness, grief and outright depression are unacceptable, we may resist. The important thing to remember is that wherever we are, however we feel, God is with us. Those who are crushed in spirit, God saves.

### For Reflection and Prayer

*Take some time to get in touch with what you were taught—by word and example—about expressions of anger, hurt, fear, sadness. What was your family's message about crying, complaining, sobbing when you were hurting? Do you remember the first time you "met" depression? What judgments did you and others around you put on the experience?*

*Write down words, phrases or perhaps images that capture your experience. Hold the paper in your hands before God if you can. With this gesture of openness, pray with everyone who is reading this book, a great community of the wounded:*

> *O God, grant us the serenity and the trust to accept what*
> *   we cannot change,*
> *the courage and the creativity to change what we can,*
> *and the wisdom to know the difference.*

# Mapping the Muddy Swamp

*God drew me out of the pit of destruction,*
*out of the mud of the swamp.* (Psalm 40:2)

Depression is not new to the human experience. We find it in the Jewish Scriptures: the melancholy of Israel's first king, Saul, and the laments of the psalmists and some of the prophets, for example. Many of those who have shaped recorded history, such as Abraham Lincoln and Winston Churchill, have at times in their lives struggled with depression. Novelists such as William Styron and Sylvia Plath, and poets such as the Jesuit priest Gerard Manley Hopkins have written while in its grip and have described it vividly. Artist Vincent van Gogh painted his depression. Handel, Berlioz, Chopin and Mahler composed their musical masterpieces with and through the agony of depression, or between bouts of its paralysis. Saints such as Louise de Marillac and Therese of Lisieux have been touched and tortured by this painful condition. Media and entertainment figures Mike Wallace and Rod Steiger have recently shared with the public the stories of their depression.

## Images of Depression

Our own circle of colleagues and clients offer a variety of images of depression. Note that some describe feelings, some thoughts, others behaviors or those attitudes that undergird behavior.

A seventy-eight-year-old woman of solid faith and quick humor describes her personal pain: "Depression for me was a many-faceted thing: loneliness, extreme sensitiveness, feeling sorry for myself, finding no joy in things I used to like...."

A middle-aged man who has been stricken with an

increasingly debilitating neurological disease offers this description: "The image of my experience of depression is that of a vacuum. Living and moving inside a vacuum becomes difficult because there are no familiar boundaries in which to gauge feelings."

A woman who has worked through incredibly painful experiences of physical and psychological abuse that left her locked in a chronic depression decribes the experience as "...chaos, being pulled in every direction yet going in no direction, an eternal state of static...a silent scream of rage."

A middle-aged woman expressed it in a prayer poem as "the straitjacket of seriousness."

Our own image of depression is based on Psalm 40. The psalmist depicts depression as a swamp:

> God drew me out of the pit of destruction,
>     out of the mud of the swamp. (*Psalm 40:2, NAB*)

The swamp of depression is abysmal, frightening, uncharted, dark; it sucks us down into death like quicksand:

> Save me, God,
>     for the waters have reached my neck.
> I have sunk in to the mire of the deep,
>     where there is no foothold. (*Psalm 69:1-2, NAB*)

If we image depression as a swamp, then a chart of its sinkholes, places of oasis and solid spots for footholds may help us map our way. First we will describe clinical depression, its biological basis and the uniqueness of each personality that makes some of us more susceptible to the disease. We will continue to offer pauses for reflection and prayer, convinced as we are that spiritual healing of depression is as important as medical and psychological healing.

## Symptoms of Depression

Each of the images and descriptions above capture a different facet of the phenomenon of depression. William Styron, in his powerful book about his own experience, *Darkness Visible*, gives voice to the paralyzing horror:

> What I had begun to discover is that, mysteriously and in ways that are totally remote from normal experience, the gray drizzle of horror induced by depression takes on the quality of physical pain. But it is not an immediately identifiable pain, like that of a broken limb.

What is depression, then, this familiar yet fearful human experience? Why, despite its widespread occurrence—as many as eleven million Americans each year—has depression been so underdiagnosed and undertreated until recently? Nathan Billig, in *To Be Old and Sad*, describes depression as "one of the great masqueraders of medicine." How many people who seek relief from sleep problems, intestinal and stomach disorders, physical pain of every variety, are in fact suffering from depression? How often does depression magnify and exacerbate genuine physical dysfunction?

While it may not be as easily identified as a broken limb, depression is most assuredly recognizable as a treatable cluster of symptoms. While clinical depression can be experienced differently in different individuals, some of its telltale signs are:

- feelings of sadness and/or irritability, more persistent than the normal up-and-down moods related to life events;
- changes in eating habits, either overeating or loss of appetite;
- changes in normal sleep patterns, difficulty falling asleep or waking up early in the morning and ruminating;
- feelings of unreasonable guilt, worthlessness, hopelessness;
- trouble concentrating, remembering, making decisions;
- unexplainable fatigue and/or loss of energy;
- restless agitation;

- loss of interest in sex and other normally enjoyable activities;

- preoccupation with thoughts of death and suicide.

These are the symptoms of one-sided (unipolar) depression, a hand that relentlessly pulls us down. Symptoms, of course, exist on a continuum. Many of us continue to function with this kind of depression. We go to work every day. We take care of ourselves and our children, more or less. But we live lives of "quiet desperation" and are unable to savor the simple joys of life. It feels like we are running a marathon in cement boots.

Therapist Martha Manning powerfully expresses her own dawning and horrifying recognition that nine out of the nine criteria for depression listed above fit her (*Undercurrents*, p. 72). She double-checked the therapists' handbook, the *Diagnostic and Statistical Manual*, and saw her own symptoms starkly outlined. Her concern for her child kept her functioning and battling intrusive, suicidal thoughts. She calls depression "the slow erosion of the self."

This is only one side of the picture. In another manifestation of depression, manic depression, a person cycles between highs and lows. Because judgment and behavior can be significantly impaired, this kind of depression is often more costly in terms of both relationships and normal functioning.

Manic depression (bipolar 1) is characterized by an abnormally elevated or expansive or irritable mood. The manic symptoms include:

- inflated self-esteem and grandiosity;

- decreased need for sleep;

- pressured speech;

- racing thoughts;

- easy distractibility;

- agitation, an abnormal increase even in goal-directed activity;

- overinvolvement in pleasurable activities that can have painful consequences, for example, buying sprees, foolish investments, sexual indiscretions, over-exercising.

Manic episodes are painful both for the person experiencing them and for family and friends. The capacity for self-destructive behavior is high in a manic episode. The more manic one becomes, the greater the potential for a crash. A severe manic episode looks much more "crazy" than the lethargy of depression. The good news is that manic depression is fairly easy to identify. Also, advances in medical treatment and in understanding the genetic links offer much hope.

Both unipolar and bipolar depression, at all levels of intensity, have a profound impact on family, friendships and work. It is hard to estimate how many families are broken up, how many careers are ruined or put in jeopardy by this disease. Because too many of us still experience depression not as a disease but a moral failing (a sin, a weak will, a stigma), too many of us resist or delay treatment. The embarrassment and shame we often feel is exaggerated by the depression itself. It seems to take control of our thought processes and paint everything in dismal colors.

Trapped in this swamp, we may struggle even to open our map. We can begin to undercut the shame so often attached to depression by first examining how our bodies contribute to the onset and deepening of depression.

### The Biology of Depression

Before we offer a simple overview of the complex realities of depression and the chemistry of our bodies, let us take a few minutes to pray. Psalm 139 proclaims that the all-loving, ever-present God knows, loves and stays with us intimately from the beginning of our existence. The unique intricacies of human life, beginning with the connections and rhythms of

all our cells and systems that develop with the union of
sperm and egg, are truly awesome. In the latter half of the
twentieth century some of the mysteries of our nerve cells
have been explored. Through advances in neurobiology, we
can better understand and find new ways to heal some of the
human suffering of depresssion.

### For Reflection and Prayer

*Let us pause to contemplate the wonders of the human body and to
pray:*

> *O God, you have probed me, you know me:*
> *you know when I sit and stand;*
> *you understand my thoughts from afar...*
> *You formed my inmost being;*
> *You knit me in my mother's womb.*
> *I praise you, so wonderfully you made me;...*
> *wonderful are your works!*
>
> *My very self you knew;*
> *my bones were not hidden from you,*
> *when I was being made in secret,*
> *fashioned as in the depths of the earth.*
> (Psalm 139:1-2; 13-15, *NAB*)

In the grip of depression, even if we cannot feel a grateful
acceptance of the wonderful mystery of our own creation, we
can ask for the grace of self-acceptance. Then we can act as if
we do accept ourselves because we believe—or are trying,
begging to believe—that God accepts us, just as we are. The
truth of our creation is that God created us as embodied
beings.

It is important to attend to those last two words: embodied
beings. Some of our former "Christian" attitudes toward the
body were quite un-Godly. God created us as embodied
spirits and found us to be "very good." The Jewish Scriptures
underscore the beauty of the body, emotions and sexuality.

When the Christian message spread through the

Mediterranean world of the first century, it rather quickly became embedded in the philosophical language of the Greeks. Unlike the Jews they had split the human person in two, teaching that we *have* a body and a soul. This set up a dualism in our budding Christian theology that often denigrated the body in favor of the immaterial "soul." In our lifetime the renewal of biblical and incarnational theology in all the mainline Churches is helping to heal that split. Wholistic spirituality reverences the human flesh of Jesus and of us as the Body of Christ. This is God's will for us. We are to be as we are created—not angels, not God, but human, embodied beings. God's will for us is peace, *shalom*, a word that means not only an absence of conflict, but wholeness, health and integrity as well. The prophet Jeremiah speaks: "Yes, I know what plans I have in mind for you, Yahweh declares, plans for peace, not for disaster, to give you a future and a hope" (Jeremiah 29:11, *NJB*).

Even while we acknowledge the wonder of our human bodies, we know that at times our bodies betray us. We will now examine the biological foundation of depression.

**The Role of Genetics.** Recent scientific studies have discovered clues about the occurrence and causes of different kinds of depression. For example, geneticists searching for hereditary links have studied multigenerational family pedigrees. In an attempt to tease out whether depression is in fact a biological or a learned phenomenon (the old "nature vs. nurture" question) they have studied twins, identical and fraternal, reared together or apart.

These studies do suggest that depression clusters in families. By examining family trees scientists find a definite genetic link. At this writing, however, the precise linkage has not yet been identified with a specific chromosome as with, for example, Huntington's disease.

### For Reflection and Prayer

*Draw a simple family tree. If you can, include your grandparents and their siblings. Ask those who have already died and who, alive*

13

*with God, care deeply about you, to look at these family roots with you. Whom can you remember as being depressed? Always or during particular years? At particular times of the year? As you mark these members of your family on the tree-drawing, take a moment or two to appreciate their pain and probable isolation. Include them in your prayers for God's peace.*

Recent scientific research opens new doors into the mystery of depression. Old mind-sets need to be rearranged. We cannot simply snap out of a low mood by sheer willpower. As with any other known genetic vulnerability (for example, diabetes, some neurological diseases and some forms of cancer), depression is a reality we need to live with and manage. Our genes are not controlled by willpower.

Genes, the givens of our bodily uniqueness, regulate the production of various proteins and enzymes that our nerves need to function properly. Genes regulate neurotransmission, which is simply the communication going on continally between our nerve cells. With apologies for vastly oversimplifying an awesomely complex process, we will look briefly at some of the neurobiology of depression.

**Our Nerve Cells and Hormones.** The most basic and simple cell in the nervous system is the neuron. How does the human system function so smoothly and coherently with its billions of cells, all of which need to communicate with one another in some kind of organized and comprehensive way? Both the nervous system and the endocrine system, which produces hormones, comprise the "communication" linkages. We experience those interior communication links as feelings, thoughts and behaviors. Biologically, however, the communication links are called neurotransmitters.

The neurotransmitters are chemicals. The two chemicals involved in depression are serotonin and norepinephrine. Both of these "brain hormones" are known to affect mood, sleep, appetite and sexual activity. Obviously, then, whether our nerve cells function properly cannot be a matter of willpower. When we are depressed, we are not malingering, nor committing that capital sin of sloth. Dysfunction of any of our hormones can produce symptoms of depression. Neurotransmitters impact hormone secretion in the endocrine system and vice versa. Mood change can be related to endocrine disorder. For example, underfunctioning thyroid mimics depression, and overfunctioning thyroid produces agitation.

A colleague and friend, Sean Sammon, a clinical psychologist and now Vicar General of the Marist Brothers' international congregation, describes in a journal article how a tumor on his pituitary gland unbalanced his endocrine system, the system that produces and regulates hormones. This malfunctioning seemed like depression. Sean writes:

> Its symptoms crept in by night, like those invasion forces that come ashore in the early morning hours before dawn. Over time they made themselves at home. Strength sapped, weight gained, mood shifted. I hardly noticed. Were there good reasons for the changes? Of course. All of them rational: too much work, too much travel, the hard coin of midlife.... How quickly illness alters life. All those plans, tied tightly in place, become undone. A move is put off, new work postponed, life reorganized. The hardest part, though, is the telling of the story. How different the reactions of people: Some become ministers and console; others avoid you, they wonder "What to say?" and speechless, wander off; still others reverse roles, making you the caretaker.... You start to keep secrets, too. After all, you were sick and didn't know it. "Why so pale?"; "My, haven't we gained weight"; "You're working too hard." Was it two years ago that the blood pressure began to climb?... "Where was I?" you wonder, "didn't I see what was happening to me?" (Sean Sammon, "Midlife Tumor," *Review for Religious*, March-April, 1995, pp. 276-278.)

Some of us might prefer the solidity of a tumor like Sean's that can be photographed and removed by surgery. The havoc on the endocrine system by neurotransmitters run amok is not visible on an MRI. Any stress, real or imagined, can flood us and change our mood.

Studies of the way we respond to stress illustrate how a perceived threat automatically precipitates a cascade of neurochemical responses throughout our bodies. These chemicals stimulate the adrenal glands to secrete a rush of adrenaline. These chemicals make us ready, loading us with energy, for the "flight or fight" response to threat. Adrenaline is essential when the threat is real and we need the extra energy. Adrenaline that is not discharged through actual fighting or running away, however, can flood our systems with feelings of anxiety, even to the point of panic. Bodily exercise can help flush away this buildup of adrenaline that goes unused. This is why exercise is always so heartily recommended for those under stress or depressed.

Neurotransmitters, like many other systems in our bodies, have a rhythm and timing that varies throughout the day. Just as body temperature, blood pressure, blood sugar and hormones vary at different times of the day, so too with the neurotransmitters. Thus, some of us experience our depression more painfully in the morning, others in the late afternoon.

Folk wisdom informs us that those who live in sunny climates appear less vulnerable to depression. Those living in a more dreary environment experience more melancholia. During the past three decades increasing attention has been paid to those depressions. They appear to be related to changes in the amount of light and are now referred to as seasonal or light-affected depression.

Light affects the release of the hormone melatonin. All of us need this hormone to get to sleep. Melatonin is produced in the dark. It depresses both our mood and agility. Each of us has an internal rhythm, our own daily biological clock, which regulates our various body systems and modulates our rhythm of rest and activity. Many people have the flexibility to adjust their body clocks to the changing environmental rhythms of the seasons.

It is hypothesized, however, that some people do not have

the automatic self-regulatory mechanisms that adjust to variations in light. As our internal clock gets out of rhythm it becomes harder to get to sleep at night or to get up in the morning. Often our craving for carbohydrates increases. The production and release of melatonin can be desynchronized. If we are exposed to bright light, the level of melatonin is reduced and therefore we have more energy. For those of us who suffer from this Seasonal Affective Disorder (SAD), therapy with light is remarkably effective. Learn to be sensitive to the seasonal variations of your moods. Ordinarily people vulnerable to Seasonal Affective Disorder experience a lowering of mood in autumn and spring, the two times of the year when the ratio of light to darkness changes.

'God's work of art.' The systems of our body manifest amazing intricacy, interdependence and balance. We are indeed "God's work of art" (Ephesians 2:10, *NJB*). However our personal chemistry functions or malfunctions, we can be sure that the one who knit us in our mother's womb stays very close. Even when we feel only God's absence, we need to recall that our creative God is at work in the most secret places of our bodies.

### *For Reflection and Prayer*

*Let us pray further with Psalm 139. Savor whatever word/phrase speaks to you.*

> *If I ascend to the heavens, you are there;*
> *if I lie down in Sheol, you are there too.*
> *If I fly with the wings of dawn*
> *and alight beyond the sea,*
> *Even there your hand will guide me,*
> *your right hand hold me fast.*
> *If I say, "Surely darkness shall hide me,*
> *and night shall be my light"—*
> *Darkness is not dark for you,*
> *and night shines as the day.* (Psalm 139:8-12, *NAB*)

## Personality Variables

Certain unique traits of personality seem to be associated with some kinds of depression. Some are genetically precoded, such as shyness. Some are the result of early mother/child interactions. Some are learned.

The impact of significant losses in a child's early years, as well as deficits in the parent/child relationship, predispose some of us to depression. Our early years are critical in establishing a solid sense of the world as a safe enough place and of ourselves in the world as solid, good enough people. Disruptions in early bonding with a mothering figure can result in an infant's being unable to differentiate feelings of anxiety and pain from its own being. Before a baby even has words, it believes "I am my feelings." This childhood distortion may persist into adulthood, leading to a belief that feelings are dangerous and uncontrollable.

Our memories from that earliest time before we had words or the ability to think are encoded in our bodies as feelings. Two common feeling memories of those vulnerable to depression are: (1) not being good enough—for example, being the wrong gender, having some handicap or even eyes the wrong color; (2) shame for feeling and expressing any or all emotion. These preverbal memories get locked—in infancy—in the "wiring" of our nervous system. These feeling memories, usually quite unconscious, become part of the "muddy swamp," treacherous sinkholes that can pull us into depression.

On the other hand, when we are babies, if we have consistent experiences of being held, tended, fed and delighted in, our budding sense of self is established in a more healthy way. When babies move into the toddler stage, little ones still need to be the apple of their parents' eyes just as they are. Parents do, however, need to frustrate gently a child's emerging grandiosity. Babies at this stage think of themselves as the center of the universe. Then reality intrudes. Toddlers bump a nose on a table leg, must share a lap with a newborn or realize they cannot control the family

18

agenda or command immediate attention. Reality and parents serve to show toddlers that they, like the rest of us, are limited. This is a tender time, between eighteen months and three years, when we begin to learn to integrate both the grandeur and vulnerability of being human and alive. Good enough—not perfect—parental love nourishes this journey. Most parents try to do their best. Sometimes their own lack of being parented makes it difficult to accept and love their own child as separate, unique and free. Certain behaviors and expressions of the child are accepted, others are shamed. As children, then, we learn to present a false self that wins approval and applause from significant adults. The true self, with all its spontaneity, creativity and variety, can be stifled and cut off, buried in our young self but never really extinguished.

As long as the split between true self and false self, the split between our masks and our real self, is not too great, there is no great harm. In fact, courtesy and tact are often the free and flexible use of the false self. If a perfectionistic, demanding, approval-driven false self stifles the real self, however, there is trouble ahead.

The false self is often expressed in covert, yet narcissistic ways. The term *narcissistic* has a bad reputation. It implies being stuck on oneself, always seeking attention, being demanding and inconsiderate of others. Sometimes others secretly render this judgment on those who are depressed, thinking them self-absorbed. There is, however, a healthy narcissism that can help to heal depression.

In the critical period of early development of the self all of us need sufficient narcissistic supplies—food for the healthy self—in order to thrive and grow. This means that we absolutely need to be the apple of someone's eye, the darling of at least one person. We need to be looked at and seen, held and cherished. We need to be mirrored. We need to see the joy in our parents' eyes as they look at us with delight. In their eyes we find the first reflection of our own goodness and worth. These are our narcissistic supplies, a fundamental and basic human need.

19

In the process of being mirrored, we are able to feel an intense bonding with at least one parent. This first crucial experience of attachment is critical for us to learn relationship skills. Without this early experience of bonding and attachment we become isolated, narcissistic adults who cannot relate to others. Paradoxically and painfully, then, those of us labeled narcissistic and self-centered have often been the most lacking in these early childhood supplies. Our early deprivation is never satisfied.

The unconditional love of primary bonding as well as the necessary frustrating of our baby grandiosities lead healthy people out of the childish need for self-centered attention. Those of us who as adults hungrily hope for some acceptance and affirmation of our right even to exist often come across as demanding, self-absorbed, using others to gratify our basic needs that we feel are never quite well enough met. This, too, is a false self. Under a mask labeled "self-centered" is the child whose true self, stomped down and split off, longs to be set free.

God gives us amazing resilience. The true self, thanks be to God (literally!), cannot be permanently killed. Consider the following story as a metaphor for this resilience. One spring day a woman accompanied her guests to their car after an afternoon visit. Her husband watched in horror as she stepped off the sidewalk and plunked a foot right on top of a crocus just peeking out of the ground. She shifted her weight as she chatted her farewells and waved goodbye. Finally she turned to go back inside. Her husband peered down at the crocus. To his amazement it was slowly straightening and reaching again for the sun. So will—so does—the true self, even after a lifetime of denial.

Consider, too, the Gospel story of Jesus' healing a woman bent for eighteen years. He sets her true self free. In calling her, looking at her, touching her, he offers her new dignity (Luke 13:10-17).

Although healing in the Gospel stories looks quick, even instantaneous, Jesus did not do magic. He would have listened carefully to the pain of those he healed. In depression we feel the pain of paralysis, of blindness, of being crippled or cast out. Jesus wants to listen to our pain as well. He will not get bored or frustrated with us when we show him again and again where it hurts. The hurt has been building for a long time, and the healing will probably take a long time as well.

## For Reflection and Prayer

*Read or recall the story of the woman who was bent over for eighteen years (Luke 13:10-17).*

*Imagine her pain, her frustration, how she must have felt cast out from the community. What brought her to the synagogue the day that Jesus was there? What did she want? What do you want from Jesus? From God?*

*Jesus calls to the woman, calls her to move forward through the segregated synagogue, through the men's section, right up to the front. How must she have felt? How would you feel? Would you go to Jesus for healing?*

*In your imagination, watch this woman move, scrunched over, protecting her vital organs, protecting her emotions. When she arrives at the front, Jesus tells her to stand up straight. Hear him tell you that whatever is twisted and damaged in you can be straightened and healed. You know that if you straighten up your vital organs will be exposed. You will feel open and vulnerable. Tell Jesus how that makes you feel.*

*Healing often hurts. As you straighten up to stand tall, your atrophied muscles scream with pain. How much easier to huddle over and hang on to your skewed view of the world. Jesus waits and watches you. Your pain and fear is etched on his face. He loves you so much that he shares these feelings with you.*

*He will wait. He encourages you to go at your own pace, to accept healing when you are ready. Even if you choose to hunch over again for years, he will wait. He will never abandon you but will surprise you, returning with healing energy in prayer times and ordinary times, in times of pain and times of peace, to offer you again and yet again the freeing of your true self.*

**Learned Behaviors.** Learned behaviors have an impact on our nervous system because they are imprinted in our nerve cells as we engage in them. Despite this imprinting they *can* be changed and healed. Depression is often the indication that such change is called for, that such healing is possible.

The attitude of entitlement is an example of a learned behavior. We are continually bombarded with advertising stimuli proclaiming that we "deserve"—a break, a Bud, the latest in designer jeans. Even our pets deserve the best. This feeling of entitlement sets us up for disappointment if not depression. When we believe that we are entitled to something, or even more tragically to someone, our disappointment when we learn we have no right to the person or thing can lead to depression. We become intolerably disillusioned by the reality of life's limits and raw edges.

A poor or fragile sense of self is often linked with depression. This, too, is in some sense a learned behavior. If once we were required to be always good, achieving, performing, if there was no tolerance of mistakes and limits, we grow up with unrealistic expectations of ourselves and others. Even if our parents have died, their expectations of us may still control our lives. Their expectations, now imprinted on our nerve cells, have become our own, and we are left vulnerable to frequent disappointment, both in ourselves and in others.

When we fail to achieve what we falsely think we are entitled to or fail to fulfill our family's and/or our own expectations of ourselves, we begin painfully to intuit that, however well masked, our life is false. Depression may grab us by the throat. The good news (which never feels good) is that depression can crack open the mask. For example, the depression that often accompanies the end of adolescence, the beginning of mid-life and the entrance into retirement from work/parenting can be a grace, an invitation to discover once again, at a deeper level, who we truly are.

**Crooked Thinking.** The way we think has a major impact on our feelings. We internalize not only parental attitudes and interactions but a way of thinking from our entire extended family. The family teaches a youngster in both obvious and subtle ways how to think about certain realities. Such training is not always healthy. Some of us, for example, are trained to become chronic worriers, learning how to catastrophize in technicolor. A flight is delayed; it must have crashed. I have a headache; it must be a brain tumor (and in its last stages, no less!).

Dr. David Burns in *Feeling Good: The New Mood Therapy* describes the various forms of crooked thinking. Because our feelings flow from how we perceive a situation, Burns considers our negative perceptions the source of much depression. Like catastrophizing, "all or nothing" thinking can magnify our worry. The tiniest flaw mushrooms into total negativity. For example, I get a B+ on my A record and so conclude that I am an intellectual failure. The quilt on which I have been working for months has a crooked seam and so I rip the whole work apart. Ruminating over the negative, yet another form of crooked thinking, involves playing and replaying a real or imagined slight or insult. Finally, mind reading is conjuring the worst possibility in the absence of evidence: Aunt Jane didn't call so she must be angry with me. My husband looks cross this morning; I must have done something wrong.

These thinking patterns are learned and their negative energy saps us. The way we see and process life triggers stress. For example, even if I only think a robber is hiding in the bushes between my car and front door, my body gets ready for "fight or flight." Adrenaline rushes, my heart pounds, my palms sweat. My adrenaline will continue to race, even though the situation is, in fact, safe. If we persistently explain reality to ourselves in negative, frightening terms, we can probably work ourselves into a fairly respectable low-grade depression. At the other extreme, however, a Pollyanna outlook will not keep us from depression. Only truth will set us free.

23

### For Reflection and Prayer

*Here is a simple prayer for healing: "Holy Spirit, teach me truth today." It is best prayed every day at the moment of waking. It is a prayer of courage.*

*A night prayer might be: "Holy Spirit, thank you for the gift of your truth today."*

Each of us feels and expresses depression in a unique way depending on our genetic coding, the chemicals linking our nerve cells, our family's experience and values, our learned behaviors and/or crooked ways of thinking. Our symptoms vary in severity. This map of depression has thus far only sketched the mud and murkiness of the swamp. Now we will examine some sinkholes in the swamp, experiences that often surprise us, gaping open like pits of destruction.

# Sinkholes in the Swamp

The ordinary muck of a swamp sucks at us continually, threatening to drag us under. Then sinkholes suddenly gape and we tumble headlong into an abyss. So it is with various types of depression. Ordinary life is full of events that can disrupt our day-to-day equilibrium. Some of these are normal developmental passages. Others are more catastrophic external events that can stretch our capacity to cope well. The Chinese character for crisis signifies both "danger" and "opportunity." We can perceive crisis in various ways. If we perceive it as a challenge then we probably feel that exhilarating surge of energy and enthusiasm that moves us eagerly to a new place. If we perceive the crisis as threat then we will probably feel the discomfort of anxiety. This physical reaction in our bodies moves us to "fight" or "flight" and floods us with adrenaline.

Perhaps the threat that most contributes to depression is the experience of loss. Loss is an integral part of being human, and we react. In this crisis, sadness is the normal feeling response. If we do not properly attend to our sadness, however, it may solidify into a reactive depression and we may find ourselves dropping into a sinkhole in the swamp.

## Reactive Depression

We don't need a genetic vulnerability to depression to experience a reactive depression. Many events in an ordinary life can leave us reeling with a sense of disorientation and loss. It may be a death or divorce. It may be the loss of a job or an experience of failure. It may be a move to a new area of the country. It may be the experience of illness or chronic debility.

Each of the normal passages in the flow of human development involves some element of loss. It may be the birth of a child, leaving home, seeing a child off to college, our own or our spouse's retirement. The aging process itself robs us of familiar and comfortable vitality. So many of these passages involve the poignant mix of genuine joy and a gnawing sense of loss. We celebrate these events, but we also need to reverence the ambivalent feelings and mourn the losses in the transition.

Our early experiences of separation and loss can make us more vulnerable to some of life's normal losses. A mother writes, for example: "I couldn't understand why I felt sad about the thought of my daughter's wedding. After all, she was marrying a real prince. Even though they were moving, it wasn't all that far away." This fifty-year-old woman eventually connected these feelings with her own vulnerability to loss, stemming from the death of her mother when she was five.

The pattern of attachment and separation occurs most dramatically during our first two years of life. This crisis is re-evoked in many subsequent experiences as we become separate persons. Serious disruptions in the attachment/bonding period of our development as infants, because of death or because of physical or emotional parental absence, leave their mark on us. We may grow up with an internal neediness that amplifies the ordinary ache of separation. We may experience a nagging doubt about our own capacity to care and to connect.

In our society, unfortunately, men especially may be shamed for this neediness. Some men keep it a secret even from themselves. A priest whose mother had been ill for most of his childhood needed a crisis to prove his ability to love. Although others knew him as caring and compassionate, he didn't feel this way about himself until a tragedy occurred: "The death of my twenty-six-year-old niece left me gasping for breath. That day I learned in a dramatic and irrefutable way that I could love and love deeply. God used my broken heart for a deep revelation."

Other events can also precipitate a reactive depression, for example, an unresolved conflict with family or friends, especially if it results in the rupture of relationship. Even the closest families are vulnerable to severed relationships. Sometimes families are too close; such families almost "need" a rupture in order to experience separateness and autonomy. Some families find separateness so threatening that normal movement toward independence can harden into permanent estrangement, a profound experience of loss.

Sometimes families have no experience or modeling in conflict resolution; with no way to deal with conflict except distance or silence, family rifts solidify into permanent divisions that pass from one generation to the next. Just as we can trace patterns of alcoholism and abuse on a family tree, so we can trace patterns of permanent estrangements. Families seem to have a formidable power to pass on unresolved patterns. So much pain gets encoded in our nerve cells from repeated slights, omissions and withdrawals; this pain can eventually lead to depression. Anger can become a defense against the hurt of a lost relationship.

Family story and history, as well as family genes, can become sinkholes in the swamp. Knowing and naming the terrain will allow us to find our way through the swamp. "One who loves them leads them." (Isaiah 49:10)

## Necessary Losses

Judith Viorst's masterful and readable *Necessary Losses* illustrates the paradox that human growth involves loss and change. She traces each of the developmental passages, each of the leavetakings that must occur for us to grow and come home to ourselves. However blissful the womb, each of us had to leave it in order to live. Birth is only the first of many leavetakings. The womb, the lap, our home, our family—life invites us to serial losses and to new attachments in order to develop as human persons.

Much attention has been paid to childhood growth and development. Less visible but no less profound are our passages through adulthood, the reassessment of our life choices in mid-life and the ultimate "amen" to our one and only life in our later years. Accepting our one and only life leads to integrity rather than to despair. Each of our choices involves roads not traveled. Choice and chance constantly reshape and refine the dreams and ideals of young adulthood. As we travel the path of our one and only life we need to come to grips with whatever disappointments life has dealt us. Bad things do happen to good people. A child may have physical or learning or behavior problems. A parent rejected by a child for whatever reason feels excruciating heartache. Misunderstanding or outright injustice can cost us our job.

Illness, our own or others', can derail dreams and rob us of skills and energies we take for granted. We often experience illness or chronic pain as a sinkhole until we learn to manage it. Our immune system is depressed. Cancer, heart disease, stroke, even the more common heart surgeries can gash open a sinkhole of depression.

Consider the stress of this middle-aged woman, wife and mother. Five years ago an unusual form of cancer left her with the chronic pain of neuropathy in her hands and feet. Ordinary activities such as walking, writing or picking things up became a real challenge. Although her cancer is cured, she has genetic reasons to worry about recurrence. A year ago, her mother-in-law, who had just moved to the area, began demonstrating signs of Alzheimer's. Now Pat and her husband watch as this sweet old lady is transformed into someone confused, testy and frustrated. Only last week Pat received the news that her own mother, a woman Pat has never related with easily, has been diagnosed with terminal cancer. As Pat prepares to bring her mother to the area to die, she also faces the reality that they may not have enough time to work through their relationship. Pat's husband struggles with depression, but her natural disposition has always been sunny and optimistic. Now, however, the cumulative effect of the stressors of these years and the challenge of managing chronic pain has left Pat with a severe reactive depression.

How many mid-life "Pats" juggle the responsibilities of the "sandwich generation," caught between the demands of growing children and aging parents, often in an environment of economic uncertainty due to layoffs and downsizing. Depression seeps in like fog. We become vulnerable to easy irritability and quick frustration. Relationships can become strained and even broken if depression is left untended.

Much has been written about "mid-life crisis." As we move through it we can experience a profound sense of loss as we review roads not taken and the consequences of our choices. One of our respondents writes:

> As I neared mid-life, I felt drained. Constantly struggling with physical symptoms, I suffered back pain that was quite debilitating. I was losing friends because I was frantically imposing on them a neediness that even I recognized as excessive. In these periods of darkness, there were breakthroughs. As a young dairy farmer I had often gathered the cows before dawn. I had experienced firsthand that only in the darkest moment of the night can the first glimmer of light be perceived. Once daylight has arrived, its power to illuminate and reveal leads me to forget that darkness will have its turn again.
>
> Spirituality for me has been that light in face of the darkness of depression. I do trust that God breaks through gradually, but as incessantly as the daylight. The ebb and flow of the ocean, the cyclical progression of New England's seasons, have called me again and again to awareness and acceptance. I am quite slowly learning to accept life's pain nearly as gracefully as life's joys. I have learned from mentors, teachers, therapists, spiritual directors and new friends that God works through all of life's processes. I have learned from God.

A word is in order here about depression and the elderly. The assumption that the elderly are more prone to depression than other age groups is mistaken. It is true that the longer we live the more losses we are likely to accumulate. We lose significant relationships—spouses, siblings, friends. We become more vulnerable to physical losses—sight, hearing, mobility. We may lose social status in our society, which worships youth. Aging, however, can also bring wisdom and enhanced gratitude for the reality of our one and only life. No evidence suggests that aging is inevitably associated with depression. Great strides have been made to differentiate between depression, mild stroke and full dementia in the elderly. Depression in the elderly is treatable and reversible, so correct assessment is critically important.

## Post-traumatic Stress Disorder

One type of reactive depression deserves particular attention. Our whole society struggles in the sinkhole of violence, and each of us has a heightened awareness of and exposure to it. Random acts of violence erode our sense that the world is a safe place. Killing fields extend beyond the boundaries of declared war zones and invade the heartland, as we saw in Oklahoma City in April 1995.

Post-traumatic Stress Disorder (PTSD), like depression, is as old as the human race. Only since the Vietnam War, however, has it been specifically identified as a mental health issue. Rising awareness of "women's" issues such as rape and spousal abuse and new revelations about child sexual abuse have made us more aware of how widespread is PTSD. This sinkhole needs some charting.

Advances in neurobiology demonstrate that stress helps to imprint memories. For example, most of us old enough to remember November 22, 1963, can recall that day with stunning precision and feeling detail. The assassination of President John Kennedy was a national trauma. It precipitated a stress reaction that locked the event in our memories.

*The Washington Post* (October 24, 1994) reported a new neurobiology study proving that the "stress hormone system" impacts how we process information. The study's findings suggest that the rush of adrenaline imprints emotionally stressful events more deeply in our memories than normal events. Sometimes the trauma is so great that it gets repressed, surfacing only in flashbacks, nightmares and other subconscious memories. The trauma may be remembered only in feeling memories of terror or depression. It may be locked in specific body memories, such as gagging, tingling or burning sensations that have no organic cause. PTSD can be disabling and almost always requires professional attention.

## Existential Depression

Existential depression is a reaction to overwhelming realities that can undermine the way we experience our world. Almost every day the media report events that can rock our sense of meaning. These constant reminders of human vulnerability and contingency can be overwhelming. The pace of change in our society threatens to outstrip our capacity to process and make meaning out of the changes. The twentieth century alone has witnessed more cumulative change than has been recorded in all of human history.

Telecommunications make us a global village, allowing us to share moments of celebration such as the inauguration of Nelson Mandela. On the other hand, we have no refuge from vivid visual images of horror. Ethnic cleansing is not an abstract theory but the tormented faces of Slavs and Africans. War is not an antiseptic, strategic game; even "smart" bombs kill real people, draw real blood, blow off real limbs and incinerate real homes. Violence screams in living color and with instant replay. We may wonder where God is in all the horror. Where was God in the Holocaust? At Hiroshima or Dresden? Where is God for the people starving in Africa? How do we begin to salvage meaning when we have such capacity ourselves to inflict torture on our brothers and sisters?

Even as we are bombarded by images of destruction, our television screens bombard us with messages designed to create new hungers and expectations. The most gruesome pictures of human suffering are interspersed with advertisements of luxury items, even gourmet pet food. The more we feed these hungers, the sharper they often become. Satiety creates boredom. The hole deep within us becomes vulnerable to addiction. Depression can deepen. "Greed is good," cried the hero of the movie *Wall Street*. Many people act on this code. Income distribution is increasingly uneven and the American Dream eludes not only the poor but even parts of the middle classes.

These realities, only briefly described, may account in part for the dramatic rise in teenage suicide. Suicide is the third leading cause of death among United States teens, behind accidents and homicide. Adolescence is a vulnerable time. What robs so many teens of hope, stifling their creativity and destroying any meaningful alternative to death? The stable family unit is becoming more rare. Rates of divorce, desertion and various family addictions continue to climb. Teens are more susceptible than adults to concerns about the world they will inherit. Some worry about nuclear annihilation, ecological destruction and dismal opportunities in the job market. The future can look bleak and meaningless.

Change has loosened some of the underpinnings that may have given people a sense of stability and meaning. Rituals and symbols, roles and rules have all been marked. The American flag is a good example of a symbol in flux. What a range of emotions it evokes in different people in differing situations: at the opening of a ball game, at an anti-U.S. rally, at a hometown Fourth of July parade, at a burial in Arlington National Cemetery.

We have ample evidence that some people perceive certain changes as a threat, for example, changes in women's roles and in the Church. Change, however, is not inevitably disorienting or depressing. As we said earlier, it depends upon our perception of the particular event. Some of the changes in rituals and roles have been life-giving, such as a new appreciation of women's gifts and energies.

Social rules change. Congress-bashing and tolerance of

verbal expressions of hatred in the media are more prevalent. Rules governing child-rearing practices and what constitutes sexual harassment have changed. Even ultimate rules about who is in charge of life's beginning and ending have changed. Theologies have changed with new insights from biblical, incarnational and Third-World theologies. God is no longer understood as remote, an unmoved being infinitely uninvolved in our human realities. The tears of God's people are the tears of God, and not one of them is lost:

> My wanderings you have noted;
> are my tears not stored in your vial,
> recorded in your book? (*Psalm 56:9*)

The pain of existential depression, like any human suffering, can transform us. If it elicits any human response of love, it is somehow redemptive. This can be an enormous challenge to our faith. Even if we are unable to touch the pain that so touches us, God honors our great desire for peace, justice and unity. Any compassionate feeling, desire, action or prayer evoked by our experience of human suffering is blessing for our world.

### The Ultimate Sinkhole

The ultimate sinkhole of depression is suicide. The first thing we need to know about suicide is that it is the most preventable cause of death. Sometimes the cumulative blows of life can be so overwhelming that we no can longer find life worth living. Depression so narrows our vision that death seems to be the only viable solution to whatever problems we encounter. Hopelessness becomes overwhelming. Listen to one of our respondents, a woman of fruitful faith who struggled with a depression so severe that it finally drove her to a nearly successful suicide attempt. She writes:

> My image of depression is like what hell must be, if
> there is one: a place of nothingness where torment
> never ends, an empty dark tomb that allows no
> escape. My dreams and any hopes for my future are

stolen from me. My thoughts become overwhelmed with negativity; no other feelings can get in. There is no place for God here because I can't let him in. My mind is overwrought with confusion, doubt and fear. How can I trust in a God who has no power to intervene on my behalf? What can I do? There is no part of me that is happy. Death is more inviting than life. I keep God at a distance, though I know he is ever present. I am afraid to build a real closeness to him. What if I let him down or he lets me down? It's safer not to risk. I must not love or trust him enough or I wouldn't find it so difficult to take this risk.

Depression exists on a continuum. What precipitates the awful descent into the tunnel vision of suicidal thinking in which death becomes the only viable option, the only solution? Richard Heckler, in the remarkable book *Waking Up Alive*, presents an extensive study of individuals who have recovered from a serious suicide attempt. For many of these, unbearable loss and alienation have precipitated the massive emotional pain that gradually overtakes them. Too often this pain is hidden behind a facade of attempting to function "normally." A withdrawal from normal activities or a gradually developing inability to function is always a signal for concern.

A fatally crooked thinking pattern holds that death is the only escape from intolerable pain. This fantasy, a sinkhole of suicidal thought and feeling, becomes our only focus. Gradually we enter what amounts to a suicidal trance in which preoccupation with death as relief becomes more and more logical and self-reinforcing. At the same time we experience an increasingly debilitating loss of will to do anything about our pain. The fantasy of death and its release becomes compellingly strong.

The warning sign we need most to attend to is the conviction of overwhelming hopelessness. God's words through Jeremiah—"My plans for you are plans of peace, not disaster. I have reserved a future full of hope for you" (29:11) —take on a special poignancy and truth. Sometimes another has to do the hoping for us. Hopelessness coupled with social isolation is a double jeopardy.

An environment where we will be safe from self-destruction may be necessary. We may need to be in the structured safety of a hospital. This environment can provide a haven where we can at last get relief from an overpowering depression.

We need to know that even this abysmal sinkhole need not swallow us up; relief is possible.

# Some Footholds
in the Swamp

In this chapter we will suggest some specific steps we might use to help ourselves recover our balance in the swamp and perhaps elude further pitfalls. If depression has paralyzed us completely, someone may have to intervene to get us proper medical attention before we can help ourselves, before we have enough energy to cooperate with God's healing action.

No matter how mild or severe our depression, when the fog has lifted enough, we can all be served by self-help techniques. As depression ebbs and flows in varying degrees of intensity throughout our lives, the self-help methods we offer as first footholds in the muddy swamp can also act as preventive measures.

Sometimes when we are depressed our inertia keeps us from trying anything. We lack the energy to find self-help books, let alone read them and work the exercises they suggest. Convinced that nothing can help us, sure that we would do the exercises wrong anyhow, we give up before we even begin.

Like Saint Paul, we say, "Who can save us from this body of death?" "Only God through Christ Jesus!" (Romans 7:24-25). We begin then by praying to the Spirit, who is the energy and power of God living deep within us, even if we do not—cannot—feel that energy. A simple "Help!" will suffice. The most certain way to solidify depression is to do nothing. Even one tiny step, uttering one desperate "Help!" moves us toward healing.

We need to make a personal commitment to our own

healing. A wide array of self-help books that deal with depression are available. Especially helpful are workbooks that directly engage us in the process of working through depression, such as *The Feeling Good Handbook* by David Burns, M.D., and *The Depression Workbook* by Mary Ellen Copeland, M.S.W.

As we outline a number of self-help steps in this chapter, start with one that fits you. Some of the strategies will suggest new ways to think about reality. Many of us get into the habit of automatic negative thought patterns. Our thinking influences how we feel. Begin to pay attention to your automatic thoughts and try to examine them rationally. If we can correct our crooked thinking patterns, we will gradually become adept at stopping some kinds of depression before they start.

Other self-help strategies involve activities. Depression dampens and distorts our anticipation of pleasurable activities and undermines our sense of competency. Our days are filled with things we need to do. Sometimes just the thought of action can be immobilizing. So we will suggest some simple ways to manage time, conserve energy and reduce stress.

We are social beings. Although depression pulls us toward withdrawal and isolation, much healing happens in community. Being able to identify and enhance our own support system is crucial for recovery.

Lastly we will attend to some of the professional resources for healing. As we have explained, most depression is biologically based. The chemicals in our brains and our endocrine system need help to regulate our moods. Because we believe that medicine is one of God's healing graces, we will encourage some medical treatments and explore various types of psychotherapy. Medicines can help restore balance to the physical system. Martha Manning, in her moving autobiographical work, *Undercurrents*, has even made the case for looking again at the healing grace possible in electric shock therapy.

## Learning to Think Straight

Perhaps no self-help tool shows results as quickly as learning to think straight. Most of us vulnerable to depression share a tendency to engage in automatic negative thinking. We know that two people can have an identical experience and yet feel quite differently about it. The way we perceive an event and interpret it to ourselves influences how we feel about it. What we think about something, what we were expecting, what the event means to us—each of these has an impact on how we will feel.

Burns, in *Feeling Good: The New Mood Therapy*, outlines some of the ways we engage in crooked thinking. Probably the most common and one of the most harmful is using a negative filter. This is a form of overgeneralization in which we pick out only the negative aspects of a situation. We dwell on these exclusively, effectively blocking out the positive aspects. A perfectionist, for example, makes one mistake and generalizes this to a feeling of total unworthiness.

Crooked thinkers tend to see reality in terms of good or bad, all or nothing. This is called splitting. An early developmental process, it loses its usefulness as we become more mature. Because it simplifies reality, many people tend to hang on to this primitive form of thinking. We recognize it as a source of fanaticism and fundamentalism, and, more drastically, as a source of mental illness and idolatry.

Another common pattern of crooked thinking is catastrophizing. We use this both when we're depressed and anxious and in order to become depressed and anxious. Sometimes catastrophizing is a form of magical thinking, such as when a child thinks: "If I think the worst, then it won't really happen." Theological magical thinking happens when we fast in order to bribe God, or open Scripture randomly to find an "answer" for a problem. It indicates how desperately we want order, certainty and absolutes to feel secure. When we cannot achieve the "answers" or rescues from our daily problems, we can become depressed, feeling betrayed by God.

Sometimes catastrophizing is a form of overgeneralizing; for example, "An airliner crashed yesterday so this plane will probably go down too." This kind of crooked thinking may simply be part of the negativity through which we explain reality to ourselves when we are depressed. Catastrophizing is always painful. Life delivers enough tragedies without our adding to them.

As a corrective to catastrophic worry we might add to the merry-go-round of our obsessive fantasizing such stoppers as these questions: "What is the worst thing that will happen if...?" or "If such and such were true, what would be so bad about that?" For example, I am racing to the train station to pick up Aunt Tillie. I ask myself: "If I am late, what's the worst thing that will happen? Aunt Tillie will turn around and go home. If that were true, what's so bad about that? Aunt Tillie will be furious and tell all my cousins I'm not efficient about time. If that were true, what would be so bad about that?" We catastrophizers need to discover creative uses for our vivid imaginations. Learning to "imagine straight" can heal so much unnecessary worry. "Fear is useless. What is needed is trust" (see Mark 5:36).

Another type of crooked thinking is personalization. We apply everything to ourselves and take responsibility for much more than reality demands. For example, sometimes children assume that Mommy's or Daddy's alcoholism must be their fault. This is another vestige of early cognitive development, normal for children, but outgrown as we become adults. At age two or three it is normal to think that the world centers on us. A three-year-old feels omnipotent, and this grandiose thinking is appropriate then. Grandiose personalization is painful, however, when it persists into adulthood.

Another grandiose crooked thought pattern is mind reading. We jump to conclusions without evidence to support those conclusions, and we act on them. For example, in adult friendships and in marriages, instead of responding directly to what we are asked, we try to anticipate what the other needs, wants or means. When partners try to read each other's minds and think they know exactly what the other person thinks, needs and wants, then miscommunication and misunderstanding abound. Sometimes we expect others to read our minds as well; "You should know that I love you" is a common cry. Deep miscommunication can ruin relationships, which then fuels grief and reactive depression. Unrealistic and rigid rules for ourselves and others can be another source of pain. Inflexible "shoulds" produce unrealistic guilt. Not only do we constantly blame ourselves, but this blaming/shaming attitude toward ourselves carries over to judging and blaming others. Our high expectations leave us vulnerable to constant disappointment, the source of much depression. If *should* or *ought* are frequent words in our vocabulary, then we probably carry the burden of unrealistic expectations.

Lastly, especially when we are feeling depressed, it is important not to confuse feelings with the objective reality. For example, I may feel like a bad person but that certainly does not make me a bad person. My feelings are not who I am. A flawed understanding of temptation and sin may have contributed to this form of theological crooked thinking. Some of us were warned from the pulpit that even to think about missing Mass on Sunday was already a mortal sin. Certainly to experience impure feelings meant that we had committed impure actions, or so some of us were taught. We cannot say often enough that feelings, emotions, desires are gifts from God, essentially good and designed for our good. They function as signals that enable us to know ourselves more fully and to make more fully human, fully free choices. Feelings clue us in to what we really want, but we are free to choose to act on the feeling or to let it pass, grateful that it has served as a signal of our deepest desires.

How can we break the habit of automatic negative thinking and start feeling better? One of our respondents has figured out what works for her. Once she is aware that she is ruminating in an unhealthy way, she acknowledges the feelings that accompany the negative thinking and then totally engages herself in an activity she enjoys. While not denying the feelings, she quite deliberately breaks the hold that her thoughts and subsequent feelings have on her.

Burns and others describe another simple technique called reframing. Suppose that in Aunt Tillie's attic you discover an original Monet painting. The beautiful scene is framed in cheap, rusting metal. We would want to change that picture's frame, no matter what the cost. Just as we constantly interpret our experiences, sometimes using crooked thinking, a new frame will surely change and may possibly enhance the picture. For example, we might say, "This is going to be a lousy day today because I got caught in a traffic back-up and was late for work." How lousy is it? Reframe the scene: "It was so sunny I could roll down my car window. I had the leisure to listen to my favorite song on the radio. A parking place opened just as I was pulling into the lot." Do you see how the negative filter is removed, revealing the ordinary mix of positive and negative in the experience?

### For Reflection and Prayer

*For this exercise to be most effective, write down your responses rather than just thinking through them. Look at this list of negative thinking patterns:*

- *catastrophizing;*

- *negative filtering;*

- *mind reading;*

- *theological crooked thinking;*

- *magical thinking;*

- *all-or-nothing thinking (absolutizing, splitting);*

- *personalizing;*

- *overgeneralizing;*

- *"shoulds."*

*Do any of them feel familiar? Naming the pattern is the first step in beginning to tame it.*

*Think of a recent situation in which you were feeling down. What was your automatic thought? Write it down. Then reframe it. For example, you might write: "I'm a terrible parent because I lost my temper." This automatic thought is an overgeneralization. To counter it, you might list the ways in which you are a good parent.*

*Instead of thinking in childish all or nothing terms, we see that we are a mix of flaws and gifts, sin and grace, not perfect but simply good enough.*

*Write a brief description of an incident in your life—long ago or quite recent. Reflect on how you interpreted the incident, how you explained the situation to yourself. Ask the Spirit of truth to help you look honestly at the event.*

*Do you note in your description that you perhaps overgeneralized? Instead of asking directly, perhaps you tried to read the minds of those involved? Was there a negative filter, some grandiosity or a "should" involved? What other realistic ways might there be to think about what happened? Write those alternatives down. See if thinking in a new way changes your feelings.*

*Use this prayer frequently:*

> *Holy Spirit, please give me the courage and the creativity to change the things I can.*

## Learning to Affirm Ourselves

If self-blame is the pattern that drags us into the muddy swamp, a simple but effective antidote is the use of positive affirmations. In order to be effective, an affirmation needs to be:

- true, short and simple;

- only positive words;

- in the first person ("I" statements);

- in the present tense.

Examples of affirmations might be:

- I am a good person.

- I can handle today with serenity.

- God loves me just the way I am.

Our faith in our loving God who accepts us just as we are can also enhance this process. The poster proclaims: God doesn't make junk. The author of Ephesians writes: "We are God's work of art" (2:10, *New Jerusalem Bible*). Some biblically based quotations offer us affirmations from God, who says to us:

- I love you. You are mine. (See Isaiah 43:1.)

- I shelter you in the shadow of my wings. (See Psalm 61:5.)

- My plans for you are plans of peace, not disaster. (See Jeremiah 29:11.)

- Come to me, you who are heavily burdened and I will give you rest. (See Matthew 11:28.)

- I am close to you, brokenhearted one. You who are crushed in spirit I save. (See Psalm 34:18.)

### For Reflection and Prayer

*Take some time right now to ask the Spirit to let some of God's affirming words to you bubble up in your mind and heart. Listen and then write down what the Spirit has said.*

*Make your own list of self-affirmations. Post them where you will see them frequently; the mirror in bedroom or bathroom is often a good place. If we speak them frequently to ourselves during the day, they help us develop positive thinking. Self-affirmations help to correct old thought patterns that have corroded our self-esteem.*

Christians can add contemplation to the practice of affirmations. Saint Teresa of Avila described contemplation as looking at Jesus looking at us, humbly and tenderly. Whenever a self-blaming thought intrudes, whenever a selfputdown triggers an obsession of guilt and shame, whenever a negative judgment of ourselves makes us doubt God's faithful kindness to us, we can look at Jesus instead of keeping our eyes fixed firmly on ourselves. Jesus always looks at us with love. We are incapable of holding two thoughts in our minds at the same time; the healing look of Jesus can take precedence over our negative thinking. We can choose his look of acceptance and treat our own self-blame as the "impure" thought that it is.

Even when we have truly sinned, our self-blaming judgment does nothing to heal us. Nonacceptance of our one and only self simply digs us deeper into misery, into the swamp. Harshness with ourselves over our failures, faults and even serious sin is not God's way; it is not the work of the Spirit. True contrition fixes our eyes on Jesus, not on ourselves and how awful we are. The Gospels assure us that Jesus comes especially for the sinner, the sick and the weak. He wants to be with us, especially when we are feeling most sinful, and even when we actually are sinful.

### For Reflection and Prayer

*Quiet yourself and ask Jesus to show you his face.*

*How does he seem to you? What emotions show in his eyes?*

*Ask him to let you know that his love and joy is in you, that you delight him. "My joy is in you, that your joy may be full" (John 15:11).*

## Managing Time and Stress

When slogging through the swamp, we find it difficult to organize time, to get started, to get finished. Those suffering the manic side of depression, on the other hand, know the racing, pressured, overextending of limits that accompanies a manic phase. Both phases need a healing balance and an intentional management of stressful stimuli.

Balance with joy our days of affliction

the years of misfortune we have suffered.
*(Psalm 90:15)*

When we are bogged down in depression, sometimes the easiest task seems too complicated and overwhelming. Then we need to be able to divide our work into manageable pieces.

Depression robs us of the simple joys of anticipation. Because we are convinced we won't enjoy doing something pleasurable, we decide not to bother. If we do start a project or even an ordinary task, depression not only makes it hard to do the work, but makes it impossible to enjoy what we are doing. The rut is deep.

A way to free ourselves from this snare of depression is to make a daily time log. Divide the day into half-hour segments. Then list what you plan to do, noting whether each task is something you have to do or something you like to do. Thanks be to God that some activities are both! At the end of the day check what you accomplished during each of the half-hour segments. If you can remember any feelings that accompanied the tasks, add those, too.

This exercise gives us concrete evidence. We all need a sense of mastery in what we do and some sense of pleasure as well. The feelings of accomplishment that have been snuffed out by depression may glimmer again, even if we can take only baby steps in carrying out our daily plan. This log also serves as an antidote to the common but overgeneralizing cry: "It's been a really rotten day. I feel so depressed."

By breaking down the activities of the morning in the following dialogue, this respondent was able to see her day more realistically.

"I felt so depressed today."

"Tell me, hour by hour, just what you did today."

"I got up, took a shower, ate breakfast, stared out the window."

"How did the shower feel?"

"Warm. Soothing."

"How did the breakfast taste?"

"We had some berries in the fridge, so that sparked up the cereal."

"What were you staring at outside the window?"

"We have the loveliest willow in the backyard and it's just beginning to get green. I was staring at this light green sway of branches. It was hypnotic, so gentle."

"When you got to work, what happened?"

"I chatted with my secretary, got a cup of coffee, finished a report. I was feeling pretty agitated so I took a fifteen-minute break and left the building. The daffodils were all in bloom."

"So what part of the morning, say in terms of fifteen-minute segments, would you call depressed?"

"Hmmm.... After I finished the report I thought of the forty-five other tasks I have before Easter and I really got both down and agitated.... I'd say about ten minutes total. But then, you see, I took that walk and saw the daffodils...."

The above example shows how dividing up the hours of the day and reframing an experience can change the negative filter and overgeneralizing tendency of our respondent.

Learning to think straight contributes greatly to being able to manage stress. Learning to manage time can also be effective. Simple time management techniques include:

- planning and prioritizing;

- breaking tasks down into small, manageable bits;

- being willing to do things "well enough" instead of perfectly;

- learning to combine activities.

Such techniques lighten the burden of time. It is especially important to include pleasurable activities in the balance of a day when we feel depressed. Maybe we have "forgotten" what we enjoy. Maybe we lack the energy to feel any joy. It is important to heighten our awareness of the ways in which ordinary daily life can nourish us. A good way to intensify our positive outlook is to focus on our five senses, our memories and our imaginations.

## For Reflection and Prayer

*Make a list now of things you like to do. Notice whether there are activities you enjoy with others as well as alone. List some activities that might increase your sense of mastery, for example, learning a new word or trying a new recipe. Pray: "Balance with joy my time of affliction, O God, just for today."*

*Rediscover wonder. Ask God for the gift of awe. Go to the window now, drinking in the beauty of the sky, perhaps a sunset, but even the ordinary clouds or shades of blue or gray. Inhale deeply your favorite scents. The pine forest in West Virginia? You can use your imagination to smell it again. Remember as vividly as you can walking barefoot on a variety of textures: lush lawn, soft sand, deep pile rug. Listen to your favorite music. Savor the taste of your favorite food tonight or tomorrow.*

### Enlisting Our Bodies to Reduce Stress

Our bodily sensations, memories and images can be the body's built-in energy givers. They rest and nourish us with beauty. We want to try to eliminate whatever drains our energy. A balanced life-style includes not only feeling and enjoying our sensations, but also adequate sleep, healthy nutrition and enough exercise.

Sleep, food and exercise can regulate mood. For example, turkey has a calming effect; tuna raises the serotonin level in our brain, thus counteracting depression. Regular exercise stimulates our endorphins, natural mood elevators within our brain. (In a manic phase, however, exercise and other stimuli need to be regulated to help us slow down.) Some health practitioners recommend twenty minutes of aerobic exercise three or four times a week; others suggest twenty minutes twice a day.

For every kind of depression, creating a tranquil environment is helpful and healing. This requires attention to light, color and sound in our external environment. If we suffer from Seasonal Affective Disorder, treatment with light can help. Our ordinary indoor lighting does not provide the full-spectrum light of the sun.

We can learn to pay attention to our breathing and to practice the healing effects of deep breathing. When we are stressed, we tend to breathe shallowly and rapidly, which deprives our system of the healthy oxygenation of breathing deeply. When we are depressed and sigh, it is not necessarily an expression of self pity; our cells are crying out for more oxygen.

We need to become aware of the tension and tightness we carry in our bodies. We can practice progressive muscle relaxation, tensing and relaxing each of the muscle groups from the soles of our feet through the tops of our heads.

Guided imagery is also helpful. Our brains and nervous systems cannot physically distinguish between what is happening in reality and what is happening in our imaginations. Thus we can create scenes of peace, success, joy, loving relationship, and our body records them as if they were reality. Our endocrine system is activated and the joy can flow. Inviting God into these scenes can deepen the peace, joy and love. The presence of God, of course, *is* reality; God lives and works and heals in our imaginations and memories.

Almost all of the good self-help books that teach stress reduction applaud the benefits of meditation, the power of images for healing, the need for a quiet time each day and a safe space for retreat. These same tools used in secular society for relaxation and stress reduction can be for Christians a kind of prayer in response to God's action in our lives. Recall that our greatest source of energy and healing is our relationship with God. We have devoted an entire chapter, "Letting God Minister to Us," to exercises that flesh out these tools. Even in the midst of our swamp, however, we can create a safe space.

## For Reflection and Prayer

*We will take an inward journey to a safe space you can create for yourself. You can retreat to this safe space whenever you feel flooded with stress.*

*In your imagination, picture a place of security, such as a spot of nature's beauty.*

*For example, image a warm sunny beach. There the sound of the ocean or lake or river lulls you with its gentle rhythm, a rhythm in union with your body's bloodstream. Let yourself feel the warmth, hear the sound. It matches your steady, deep breathing and heartbeat. Rest there.*

*Trust that in this secret place deep within you the Spirit breathes and keeps you safe. You can always return here when fears, anxieties or griefs threaten to overwhelm you. Any time, any place, you can retreat to your interior safe space.*

## Building Support Systems

We all need people who can accept us the way we are. We need people who can listen, affirm, play with us, challenge us. Often these people are family members, friends or colleagues. Sometimes when we are depressed we withdraw from the people who care about us. We may lack the energy to be with people. Or we may be convinced that no one wants to be around us. Sometimes shyness or lack of self-confidence can lock us in isolation. Sometimes we are exhausted from being over-responsive to others' needs and wants. When we neglect caring for ourselves and withdraw, we may be blocked from asking for the help we need.

One of our respondents finally realized she was neglecting herself and overworking, all in the name of service to the local Church. She wrote:

> For me, burnout was a danger. Colleagues, friends
> and family expressed concern. I, however, felt
> confident that God would continue to work marvels
> through me. Despite my sincerity, my focus
> increasingly became skewed and blurred. A series of

relationships were doomed to painful death because of my codependence, patterns of service that consumed me rather than becoming mutually nourishing.

Another of our respondents wrote of her safe space, a kind of "holding environment" whose boundaries make her feel secure:

> Friends and family provide a holding environment and affirm my goodness. Relationships challenge my "life-is-empty" point of view. With alcoholism on both sides of the family I suppose my depressive traits have a biological grounding. I try not to turn in on myself, but immerse myself in the reassurance of those close to me as if their hope is my hope. Until I can rebuild my own sense of hope and groundedness, I am holding on to others for dear life—literally. Hope is therefore concrete, touchable, right in front of me so I can't miss it. During these times, God-talk feels quite empty to me. People, however, are very real for me.

Not all of us are scintillating conversationalists, but during times of depression we may especially feel that we bore others or are not good listeners. It is often as hard to listen as to ask directly for what we need. Learning to request rather than demand, learning to be realistic in our expectations of other people, can be helpful communication skills. Support groups can teach us simple skills of communication and interaction. Many cities and towns already have established self-help support groups for those suffering from depression, whether unipolar or bipolar. While group therapy can also be helpful, these self-help groups are free of charge. It is important to check their appropriateness and personal "right fit." If no group operates in your area, Copeland's *The Depression Workbook* provides some simple guidelines for forming a support group.

Many of us have found the comfort and companionship of a pet immensely helpful. Scientific research has already recorded the beneficial effects of pets for people with hypertension, for people recovering from cardiac disease, for residents in nursing care facilities. Pets provide the safe comfort of touch. Pets can elicit our sense of responsibility; they need our care, which can pull us away from our pain. Finally, we cannot recommend strongly enough a "heavenly support group." Our dear ones who have died surely continue, with Jesus and our favorite saints, to make intercession for us. With God, they too are close to us, their brokenhearted loved ones. Even if in some way they once contributed to the crushing of our spirit, now they see us clearly and love us without reserve.

### Medical Grace

> Honor the physician...
> God has established this profession,
>  giving the doctor wisdom...
> God makes the earth fruitful with
>  healing herbs which the prudent
>  will not neglect...
> Through which the physician can ease pain
> And the pharmacist can prepare medicine.
> (*Sirach 38:1-2, 4, 7*)

*Therapy* comes from a Greek word that means healing. Because of depression's biological base we attend to medical forms of healing, therapies that directly address the biology of depression. Significant breakthroughs in treatment have taken place in the last few years. The complexities of depression have not been completely unraveled, but enormous strides have been made in its healing. The effects of some of the newer antidepressant medicines have been for many of us a genuine "medical grace." These medications are able to set free those of us who are snared in the terrifying trap of depression. Antidepressants can allow us to begin to enjoy that life in abundance that is God's will for us.

Many of us may resist taking medicines for depression, despite their healing potential. We need to look at what taking medicine means to us. Is it an admission of failure, of lack of will power? Yet depression can no more be willed away than can diabetes. Does it mean that if we take medicine we must be really sick, mentally ill? We would not make the same judgment about those who take insulin. Are we afraid of becoming addicted? Antidepressants are not addictive and are used by recovering alcoholics. Do we fear the side effects? Doctors, especially psychiatrists and psychopharmacologists, can help us identify any of these side effects and counter them. Most of the side effects are temporary and are not nearly so disabling as depression. Will antidepressants be costly? Again, physicians can address these financial concerns by prescribing older, yet effective antidepressants which, in generic form, are not too expensive.

Finally, this brief word about the biological effects of Electroconvulsive Therapy (ECT). Much controversy has surrounded this treatment. It has been moderated and made much safer in its application. The punitive images of ECT portrayed, for example, in the movie *One Flew Over the Cuckoo's Nest*, based on the book by Ken Kesey, can make people fearful of a treatment that has been considerably refined. Manning's recent account of her personal experience of ECT in her book *Undercurrents* testifies to its lifesaving value.

**Psychotherapy**

"Honor the physician," Sirach's wisdom counsels. Many professionals are trained to offer psychotherapy, and some are licensed physicians. At this writing, only medical doctors in the United States can prescribe antidepressants. While some general practitioners suggest and monitor antidepressants, psychiatrists are medical doctors who specialize in treatment of depression and its physical components. Some psychiatrists offer psychotherapy, "talk therapy," in conjunction with their monitoring of medicine. Others take enough background information to prescribe wisely, but let clients continue talking with a trusted psychologist, clinical social worker or pastoral counselor.

We make a distinction between counseling and therapy. Simply expressed, counseling is the helping relationship in which clients can discover new strategies for freedom and real love in their various and usually current relationships. When depression is a factor, a brief type of counseling such as cognitive therapy or behavioral counseling may be useful. Cognitive therapy examines patterns of crooked thinking and strategizes new ways of interpreting events, new ways of explaining life to ourselves. Behavioral counseling examines our painful or self-defeating ways of acting and may coax us to "act as if." By changing our behaviors we often can deal directly with depression.

Psychotherapy is a longer, deeper process. It may integrate any of the healing methods of the cognitive or behavioral strategies. Pastoral psychotherapy includes the spiritual dimension of healing. Psychotherapy, as practiced by a well-trained and licensed clinician, uncovers the self in order to change deeply rooted and often unrecognized patterns of thinking, feeling and behaving. This psychodynamic, therapeutic relationship with a therapist provides a "holding environment," a safe and well-boundaried space in which we can gradually uncover old and festering wounds to our spirit. This holding environment can contain our rage, grief and panic as we work through them: feeling them, talking about them, naming and claiming the pain of our lives. In the therapist's office, our deepest emotions can come into the light; when this happens, hearts and relationships begin to heal.

Long-term therapy is called for when we have experienced serious deprivation or trauma, for example, war or childhood physical and/or sexual abuse. While the shorter term therapies that focus on problem solving and behavorial or interpersonal changes are extremely helpful for depression, trust is often fragile if we have been deeply wounded. The trust—in ourselves and in God as well as in the therapist— necessary for any depth of self-exploration usually takes time to develop. Our growth in freedom and the restructuring of a pain-filled personality also calls for time, patience and long-suffering.

As one of our respondents, a clinical social worker who struggles with her own depression expresses it: "Psychotherapists try to create for their clients a safe environment where clients can feel and express their deepest selves. They are 'held' emotionally as they gain strength and the skills to expand both their understanding of life and their responses to it."

Each profession in the mental health field—psychiatry, psychology, clinical social work, professional counseling, pastoral counseling—has its own training and credentialing process. You may have to interview several therapists in order to find the right one for you. Professional and technical competence are important. Equally important is your comfort level with the therapist's caring, and intuitive trust in the therapist's ability to journey with you toward healing of your deepest self.

One of our respondents says this of therapy: "During depression I have a different experience of God. God at those times is not 'spirit'; rather God becomes very tangible in the people who tend me."

# Mourning to Morning

*At dusk weeping comes for the night;*
*but at the dawn there is rejoicing.* (Psalm 30:6)

More than a foothold, grieving can provide a boardwalk through the muddy swamp of depression. Mourning the losses of our life is a longer process than simply grabbing a temporary hold. While the muck oozes all around, we can keep a surer footing on these planks that wind through the swamp. Dealing with loss and unresolved grief is one of the ways to heal much depression. Grieving, paradoxically, can be good.

Loss is a universal experience. Losing a loved one to death might be one of the most painful experiences of human life. Yet no one who lives long enough can escape its pain. Not to grieve our loss in as unique a way and for as long a time as we need can put us at risk for depression as well as other physical illnesses. Thus, painful as it is, expressing our grief is good. Grieving is necessary.

Not all loss is as permanent and physical as death. Divorce, the death of a marriage, is often said to be more painful than physical death. We may watch sacred symbols shatter, or search for an identity stripped from us by mid-life, old age, sin or illness. Job loss, estrangement from a loved one, an unsought retirement, geographic separation can trigger a grieving process as painful as that which death evokes. In loss, our former identity is tortured, dies and is buried. But if we bury our grief, it lives underground and can reemerge as physical illness and/or chronic depression.

Grief is multifaceted. Physically, pain and tightness can

make us feel as if the center of our chest is gripped with fire, as if our heart is actually broken. The stress of grief can weaken our immune system. Psychologically, the pain is exquisite and seems interminable. Spiritually, we may cry, "Where is God?" Socially, our world is temporarily shattered.

Our fast-forward society does not always reverence the time needed for the important work of grieving. We are expected to "get over it" and to get on with the business of living. The reality is that for us things will never be quite the same again.

What is grief, this natural consequence of loss? This most common yet most unique of human experiences is not a simple emotion. It grips our body, our mind, our psyche. It changes forever the contours of our social world. And it hurts, hurts, hurts—breath-grabbing pain that sneaks up like an intruder at the most unexpected times and places.

Next to birth and death, grief over loss is the most universal of human experiences. Loss is the eventual and inevitable outcome of all our human attachments: the necessary, the helpful, the addictive and the idolatrous. One would think that an experience so much at the core of life would become easier to tolerate with practice and frequency. Not so. Nothing can totally insulate our hearts from the scalding pain of losing someone we love.

Loss can be real, tangible, as close as a spouse, a child, a parent, a friend. It can also be symbolic. Loss of a job, loss of one's place in society, loss of reputation or identity—any of these can snare us in a grief that demands to be honored.

The grieving process, despite its universality, has been studied for only about fifty years. Erich Lindemann's (1944) work with the survivors of the Coconut Grove fire victims in Boston remains a classic and landmark study. It identified both the bodily and psychological outcomes that accompany grieving. Only twenty-five years later did the British physician Colin Parkes do extensive research with widows and widowers. He identified even more closely the phases of the grieving process.

C. S. Lewis in *A Grief Observed*, his poignant journal

following the death of his beloved wife, Joy, gives an intimate picture of one man's pain. He wrote:

> No one ever told me that grief felt so like fear. I am not afraid, but the sensation is like being afraid. The same fluttering in the stomach, the same restlessness, the yawning. I keep on swallowing.

Our culture offers little support to those who mourn. True, some churches and hospitals offer bereavement support groups. The hospice movement has been compassion enfleshed. Yet our society at large still denies death and its impact on the bereaved. Few traditions have survived to show when we are mourning. No more black armbands or widows' weeds to signal wordlessly that we are grieving. Christian rituals of mourning are brief. They usually occur in the immediate aftermath of death when we are ordinarily numbed by death's impact. In our society we have lost our sense of death as the natural and integral outcome of life, as central to the human process as birth and growth.

## Factors That Impact Grief

Before noting the phases of the grieving process, we will consider some of the factors that may intensify the process. Certainly the closeness of the relationship with the lost loved one or the importance of a shattered symbol is central. How long and intense was the relationship? What was the quality of the relationship? Any genuine human attachment is marked by ambivalence, but if there is guilt or unresolved anger toward the lost one or about the loss, it can complicate our grieving.

The circumstances surrounding the death or loss also impact grieving. If we have watched a loved one be tormented with pain and diminishment, death may feel like a blessed relief. Grieving has happened along the way as our loved one's life is gradually whittled away by illness or aging. But sudden, traumatic or untimely death is another story. There is something almost obscene about a twenty-six-year-old mother dying of flu, or a vital young man being killed in a car crash. Sometimes a person's death may also carry a stigma, for example, death from suicide or AIDS, which intensifies and complicates the survivors' grief. Our personalities impact how we grieve, as do our prior losses. Our support systems also make a difference—for good or ill. Families and friends can be present in a helpful way or in an unintentionally intrusive or destructive way. If the person who has died has been the hub of the family there is an additional impact. Families are ordinarily the ones to whom we turn first for basic needs and support. At the time of a death or divorce, however, family members are simultaneously more in need of support and less able to deliver it. Feeling more needy and more depleted, family members can unintentionally hurt or fail one another. Grieving is a tender time for all.

## Stages of Grief

Although no one is a stranger to grieving, we will begin here by outlining its phases. Building on the influence of Elisabeth Kübler-Ross' book, *On Death and Dying*, we now know that good evidence suggests that grief is more uniquely personal than her five stages may suggest. We each do our own grief work in our own way and according to our own timetable. There is no recipe for "doing it right." Grief demands that we live into and through it.

We can recognize, however, common stages in the grief process. Initially, grief over any loss is usually accompanied by numbness and shock. The impact of any shock, whether physical or emotional, temporarily numbs our system, which cannot take in the full impact. This numbness mercifully protects us somewhat from the assault. In the days immediately following a death, for example, often we are like robots. Shock keeps us temporarily distanced from the reality even as we move through the rituals that mark it.

Although our emotions may be numb, our bodies react with physical symptoms that combine the body pain of anxiety and depression—dry mouth, sighing, muscle weakness, trembling, weeping, poor sleep, loss of appetite. We have little energy available for others. Like depression, grief consumes energy. It is hard to think about anything other than the deceased. The feelings that do arise are painful. Family and friends may help by sharing stories that evoke memories of the person we have loved and lost. Expressions of sympathy, flowers, Mass cards, casseroles and cakes—each symbolizes an attempt to be with the grieving one.

Usually not until after the wake and the funeral, until after friends and family have scattered, does the stark and empty reality hit. The second phase of bereavement is marked by the searing awareness of loss. As those who have come to console return to "business as usual," we who grieve may find it impossible to escape not only the acute pain but the mental disorganization that accompanies the devastation of loss. Because enduring stress weakens the immune system we are most at risk for illness during this time. The emotions of this phase require a great deal of energy.

During this phase we can be wracked with a variety of painful feelings. The awful ache of missing the person and yearning for his or her presence seems overwhelming. Songs, objects, memories, even smells can evoke a flood of emotion. Especially with the death of someone with whom we have shared the ordinariness of daily life, there is the half-conscious expectation to see the person in a favorite chair or engaging in a special activity. During this time crying is both helpful and healing. Rather than trying to close the floodgates, we need to let our tears flow. Unshed tears will exact their toll in other ways—illness, physical pain, irritability.

We can be torn with "negative" feelings at this time, for example, anger at the person for leaving us, or anger at the physician who couldn't heal. The anger and guilt we direct toward ourselves for not doing more can be the most painful, especially with death or divorce. Endless scenarios of "if only..." crowd our minds with recrimination and accusation. Sometimes we can even feel guilty for being the one to survive. This is especially true with the death of a child.

Psychological aspects particular to this phase of grieving are often aggravated by sleep disturbance. If we have never before experienced the disorientation of grief, we may feel crazy. We can be hypersensitive during this time. Akin to the irritability of depression, this sensitivity can be confusing both to ourselves and to those around us. Even if we are normally even-tempered, we can become short on patience and overreact to real or imagined slights. "Depression seems like tiny blazes breaking out all over the forest, about to consume acres upon acres in one huge conflagration," one of our respondents said to explain her irritability after the death of her mother. This can puzzle our friends and family, unaccustomed to this unusual touchiness.

Many people who study grief have observed that during this time the bereaved find themselves searching for the deceased. This may be expressed, for example, in frequent visits to the cemetery, or in wearing an item of clothing belonging to the deceased. One person reports the comfort of burying her face in her deceased husband's clothes in the closet. Another speaks of the aching moment of recognition that the person in the car in front of her is not Dad, even though from behind the shape of his head is identical.

Accompanying the searching and yearning is often a sense of the presence of the other in signs or dreaming. Both comforting and painful, these feelings often coexist with an ongoing sense of disbelief that the person is really gone.

This phase of grieving is a time of emotional storm and arousal. Our systems can endure that for only so long. Finally exhaustion takes hold. Eventually prolonged stress leads to literal or figurative collapse. Energy expended must be replenished. Only by a kind of energy conservation and withdrawal, usually with extra sleep, can we recover. This phase of grieving mimics depression. Both rob us of energy; often a kind of hibernation is required to regain energy and hope.

During this period of exhaustion and rumination, we may feel as though things will never improve. A seventy-eight-year-old woman, who lived with her only sibling, reported waking up in tears early every morning from the time he died. Each successive holiday, which had once been a time of fun and celebration, became a torment. She went over and over in her mind the details of the days before her brother's death. Obsessed with questions about the quality of his medical care, she reviewed endlessly the course of his treatment.

A friend crushed this woman's fragile spirit by suggesting that taking such a long time to grieve showed her lack of faith. "No," she argued after she had prayed through this new pain. "I read and reread the psalms. I would say that my faith is deepening." Another friend suggested that her attachment to her brother might border on idolatry. Not so. Again, her deep attachment to God taught her this truth: God is not in competition with our many loves. Rather the good news of the Incarnation is that God is present, active and loving us through all the healthy love attachments of our lives.

During the time of pain-filled thinking and powerful emotion we do the necessary grief work. There is no short cut, no fast forwarding the process. Each of us has a different timetable. To stifle the process could invite clinical depression or physical illness. The core of grief work is, first, coming to grips with the reality of the loss, and second, dealing with the seemingly myriad changes set in motion by the loss.

The elderly certainly suffer multiple losses. Continual mid-life losses, too, strip us of so much that gave us our first identity: ambitions, ideals, children and/or parents, images of God, meaning, sometimes spouses, work, home.

Children, too, need to grieve, and grieve, not alone, but in the community of the family. They are most impressionable, so the family rules and myths about grieving often cripple them in later life.

### For Reflection and Prayer

*What were the spoken and unspoken rules in your family of origin about loss? About death? Did your family mourn together or in solitude? What was healthy about your family's grieving? What was unhealthy? Did you ever dare to break any rules or discover some unspoken truths?*

The following story includes the debunking of a myth/rule of silence by a girl and her equally grief-stricken father. It is told by a middle-aged woman who was not allowed to grieve her losses in childhood. These separations left her—even after therapy—unable to break through a life of depression and separation anxiety, until the right antidepressant medicine finally broke the cycle. "Was there ever a time when I wasn't depressed?" she asks.

> Yes. I can remember with great vividness the little girl who loved to ride her trike and explore every cranny of our quiet neighborhood. One of my most vivid memories is of hollyhocks—their fragrance, color, unique texture. My capacity to savor and enjoy indicate that I was not depressed then.
>
> My mother died when I was born. A warm extended family, a doting maiden aunt and an incredibly caring foster Mom, I thought, compensated for the loss from which my father never recovered.
>
> Daddy lost his own mother when he was fourteen. His grief drove him to depression and withdrawal and he dropped out of school at the time. Economic realities of the Great Depression prolonged his courtship with my mother, his beautiful Rose. They were married only ten months. I was born prematurely. My mother died from the complications of toxemia three days later. My father grieved that death until his own seventeen years later.
>
> In retrospect I can identify some of the dysfunctional rules for grieving in our family. They probably converted what might have been painful but normal mourning into a leaden depression. My dad's family did not show their grief except by stoic silence.
>
> This silence hardened into well-intentioned proscriptions about ever talking about the dead.

Consequently, until recently, there has been a real void in family stories. As a child I understood clearly that I was never to talk about my mother because "your daddy will feel bad." So my questions and curiosities were crowded into trips to our attic where I spent hours poring over the meager treasures in my mother's hope chest. There were also occasional violations of the family rule. Ironically Daddy would answer my questions about my mother, usually during the Friday TV show "I Remember Mama."

Could I have escaped the depression that burdened our home? Was it genes or multiple losses and unresolved grief that locked me into the bleak landscape of depression where joy became an effort and gray fog settled everywhere? Probably a combination of both. Losing my mother as a premature infant meant a three-month stay in a hospital incubator. At that time it was not well understood how crucial holding and touching are to a newborn. When I was sent to boarding school I was expected to behave and certainly not show the wild terror I felt in this new environment. Books became my new caretakers.

Studying and learning became my refuge. Even that joy, however, evaporated at Daddy's sudden death when I was in high school. "Don't cry. Don't talk. Don't grieve." A good road map for grief to take a right turn into depression.

We hope children today are more encouraged to express their mourning than this woman was. Another of our respondents writes of her young granddaughter's spontaneous grief:

Four-year-old Amanda had watched her mother collapse with an aneurysm on Christmas Eve. This was a family too familiar with death but a family that knew how to grieve. The next Christmas Amanda's main request from Santa was to bring back her Mommy. When, as the youngest in the family, she was asked to bless the family meal on Christmas day, her clear prayer was "Bah humbug!"

This child was able to express a range of feelings within her family. She will grow up deeply wounded, yet, one hopes, unscarred by the depression that is bred of unresolved loss.

## Turning Point

Eventually grieving reaches a turning point, a decision either to move forward with life, even in the darkness, or to embrace the status quo, even if it means giving up on life. Up to this point, grieving has a biological as well as an emotional reality. The biological reaction to shock that triggered the cascade of anxiety has run its course through exhaustion and withdrawal.

Now we need to feel, not bury, the pain. Then we need to talk about our loss. Feel and talk, feel and talk. Rage and cry and feel and talk. Whimper and sleep and feel and talk. We do not need to eat more, smoke more, drink more alcohol or make any major decision. We need to feel our loss and talk about it, explore it, pray our feelings, laying them all, just as they are, before God.

Finally, if someone has heard our pain, receiving it with all its raw edges, if we have known that God cares most tenderly for us in this brokenhearted and crushed state, we can gradually move on. Healing begins to happen. Tentatively we begin to feel it, although we may not yet realize that the entire painful process has all been part of the healing.

To move beyond grieving calls us to a new sense of ourselves. We learn to let go of the old familiar roles and rules. We may embrace a new identity. We feel better physically as our immune system bounces back, sleep becomes more regular, energy slowly returns.

This is a time for forgiving, for letting go. It is time to forgive ourselves for what we think we did or did not do, for what might have been, accepting our one and only self. It is a time to forgive the person who has died or divorced us or fired us. Remember, however, that we do not forgive by an act of the will, but by the gradual grace and gift of God.

It is a time to forgive God, even if our intellect assures us

God didn't "take" our loved one or "test" or "chastise" us through this loss. Loss and death are part of life. Even Jesus tells the disciples on the road to Emmaus, it was "necessary that the Messiah should suffer these things and enter into his glory" (Luke 24:26). It was not necessary for Jesus to suffer a bloody death, but Jesus needed to experience a full humanity, which includes dying.

One fruit of successful grief work is a new sensitivity and deeper compassion for those who suffer any kind of loss. Our experience shows us that many "necessary losses" accompany the passages from infancy and childhood through adulthood. Our attachments and leave-takings are part of forming a self and a family or community of our own. From the most painful losses of death and divorce to normal and minor transitions, each must be grieved. Grieving suffuses reality. "The world is charged with the grandeur of God," the poet Gerard Manley Hopkins says. Undoubtedly it is also charged with the grief of human beings. God understands, and catches each one of our tears.

### For Reflection and Prayer

*List some of your own losses, both old losses and more recent ones. How has each changed your life? Who or what has been helpful to you during these times? Share your feelings with God.*

## Anniversary Reaction

Mourning provides a long boardwalk through the swamp. Waves of grief will flood us from time to time during the first year of any loss, and will often continue for years to come. Because the shock of a loss numbs us, often a surge of painful feeling surrounds the anniversary of the loss, particularly a death. The first anniversary usually finds us just sensitive enough again, just feeling enough again, to bear the brunt of grief in full. One of our respondents, a fifty-five-year-old woman, offers this example:

Every October my family gets a little apprehensive. October thirty-first is the anniversary of both my grandmother's and my father's death. My grandmother died in the 1918 flu epidemic. Her two youngest children never got over it. Her youngest, my Aunt Ruth, talked about her mother's death until the day she died. My Dad had been sickly as a kid and close to his mother. The family really freaked when he died of a flu-like illness on Grandma's anniversary, October thirty-first. He was exactly the age she had been when she died.

His sister, Ruth, lived to be eighty-four. During her last illness she talked incessantly about losing her mother. We were spooked but not surprised when she became very ill a couple of days before Halloween. I was amazed that she lived through that day. I don't know why it surprised me then that she died three days later, on the anniversary of her father's death!

The first anniversary of a loss, and particularly a death, can be more painful than the actual experience. During a wake and funeral, we often are protected by numbness. We "get through it." A year later (and perhaps eight or thirty years later) we are grief-stricken afresh, and with even deeper feeling. One year or many years later our emotions invite us to "work it through": feel and then talk about both the feelings and the loved one. We can especially speak directly to "those who have gone before us in faith." We are a people who believe in the resurrection, that our loved ones are very much alive. Often the grief-stricken find it easier to communicate with those who have died, just because of this belief. The dead person can know, understand, accept and love us as perhaps she or he never could while on earth. Reconciliation can happen. Relationships can continue and actually deepen.

### For Reflection and Prayer

*Take some time to reflect on your own family. List all the death dates you know. How wide do you cast the circle of loss throughout*

*your extended family? Focus on each person, one at a time. Try to
feel your feelings.*

*Share them with the person who has died, using direct address.
For example: "Daddy, I miss you so much...." "Marty, I'm so sorry
I didn't come to your wedding...." and so on.*

*Do you feel or intuit or hear any response? Ask these family
members to pray for you and with you now.*

We are not alone on this boardwalk through the swamp. Our
God and our community of saints who have gone before us in
faith stay with us in our process of mourning. So too does a
living, breathing, tangible community, even if you have just
one friend or helper. After mourning comes the morning, and
"at dawn there is rejoicing" (Psalm 30:6).

# Lifting the Burden

A chart through the swamp may help us to recognize depression and to turn for help before it gets a choking hold on us. In Part Two we turn to God for help; we discover God's hope for us, God's promise of shalom. We have described in Part One the physical, mental, emotional and spiritual pain of depression. Depression may spring from our genetic makeup or physiology, from misfiring neurons in our brain, from patterns of crooked thinking and buried emotion, from losses of various types and degrees. Sometimes loss includes the loss of religious symbols, institutions, meaning and even the seeming loss of God.

How will God share this burden of depression with us? God responds: "I took a heavy burden from your backs" (see Psalm 81:7).

When God takes the heavy burden of depression, it is usually not a rescue. Sometimes it hardly even seems a relief from the pressure. God's "taking" the burden most often means that God shares the burden with us. Jesus invites us: "Take my yoke...for my yoke is easy and my burden light" (Matthew 11:29-30). Yokes are made for two. We are yoked together in this suffering, yoked with God, yoked with Jesus.

Historically Jesus did bear the burdens of the sick and despised of his country for the few short years of his life. In his risen life, his risen body, he bears the burden of all peoples at all times. His presence today is no less real than it was in the first century in Galilee. He continues to bear our burdens with us, making intercession for us before the face of God (see Hebrews 7:25).

Jesus learned from God how to bear burdens. The Psalms tell us: "Our God bears our burdens day after day" (Psalm 68:19-20). This is a remarkable statement about our God. The Israelites proclaimed that their God was different from the gods of their Canaanite neighbors. Most of the gods of the other cultures were a demanding lot, asking for a demeaning, placating submission, even human sacrifice. Our God, however, is a burden-bearer.

## A New Kind of Parenting

We have not always known that our God bears our burdens. Many of us feel that God is a burden-giver. Pain, sickness, suffering, failure, disappointment, agony and general wretchedness are still sometimes attributed to God by our preachers, teachers or our own crooked thinking.

We may have been taught that God uses a variety of sufferings to test, discipline and strengthen us. This is hardly *good* news, that gospel criterion we use to measure our Christian living. We may forget (or may not have known) that Scripture does not record absolute truth; rather it documents the religious experiences of the authors, experiences that were conditioned by their culture. Their experiences of God were conditioned by their images of God. Like us, they may have projected their own human experiences of love and hate, welfare and war, anger and justice, work and worthiness onto God.

Chief among biblical images of God is that of parent. Like us, the biblical authors may have projected their experience of being parented onto God. Parents, as most of us have experienced, "discipline" their children. Unfortunately, we have lost the root meaning of *discipline*, which is learning. Parents often focus so much on teaching, training and forming their children that they fail to learn who they are, what their potential might be. The training too often is parental control. Rather than stand in awe at the mystery of their budding personalities, we try to shape and form, reform and conform them. We "discipline" them—all for their own good, of course.

*For Your Own Good* is the title of an indictment by Alice Miller of child-rearing practices. A Swiss child psychiatrist who was interested in how Hitler could rise to power, she researched the manuals of discipline used by German parents in the decades before the Hitler phenomenon. She has shown that cruelty to youngsters breeds in them a way of identifying with their persecutor parent(s) so as to gain approval and even love, so essential for a child's survival. They grow up to inflict the cruelty they received on their own children, "all for their own good."

Who will break this cycle of violence? Who will stop the crushing of the child's spirit with its resulting depression? God who bears our burdens day after day! This is the Good News. The Law came through Moses, but grace and truth, God's unconditional love and faithfulness, have come through Jesus Christ. God's love is unconditional, not cruel. God trusts us and does not control us. God's action saves us, sets us free, gives us space and time to become who we choose to be. God, as revealed in the person of Jesus, is never cruel or violent.

We who have the gospel, who are disciples (learners), need to learn this Good News of our God. The Spirit continues to inspire us, the Church, to discover new images of God. The Spirit can break down the way we project onto God our own experience of being parented. The Spirit is healing right now.

### For Reflection and Prayer

*Take some time right now to respond to the Spirit's healing energy. If as a child you were spanked, slapped, ridiculed or ignored, offer the Spirit your wounded little child's heart. How will you image the Spirit's healing force? Will it be a gentle breeze caressing this young heart? A swirl of refreshing water? A hand tenderly stroking the bruised places?*

*You may feel like crying. The Spirit is a fountain of living water welling up from deep within us, John's Gospel claims. Let the Fountain-Spirit flow.*

The tears of God flow. God shares our burdens. God cries with us. Through the prophets, teaches Rabbi Abraham Heschel, God gives voice to the people's silent agony:

> Oh, my head is all water,
>     my eyes a fountain of tears,
> I weep day and night
>     for the slaughtered of my people!
> (Jeremiah 9:1)

God bears our burdens. Not only does God not burden us, God does not test us either. Do spouses who have a vibrant relationship make up little tests to prove the other's love? When we notice ourselves questioning and testing another's love, we need to use such crooked thinking as a signal to talk straight to ourselves before we become mired in emotions of distrust, sadness and/or anger. If we try to trust and not test those whom we love, how much more God would trust and not test?

God bears our burdens day after day. Our God is a God who saves. Our God is like a parent who sets us free to become our true self, springing up from deep within.

## Plans for Peace, Not Disaster

God's will for us is that we not be burdened. God's will for us is that we be free. God's will for us is shalom, our peace. The Hebrew word *shalom* means so much more than absence of conflict. It also means wholeness, health and integrity. It means integration of body and spirit, a wholeness of the person.

"My plans for you are plans of peace (shalom) and not disaster. I have reserved for you a future full of hope" (Jeremiah 29:11), God promises through the prophet Jeremiah. In the Jewish Scriptures, God puts all of the divine energy into easing burdens, removing the chains of slavery, providing personal and political freedom for this beloved people.

In Jesus, the New Testament evangelists assure us, our

burden-bearing God has come close to us. Jesus is eager to use all his energy to heal pain, sickness, suffering, failure and general wretchedness. In his teaching Jesus offers ways of shalom. "Happy are you...blessed are you...be compassionate as our Father is compassionate...forgive...love one another as I have loved you...wash feet...." To see Jesus in action is to see God's compassion in the flesh; to hear Jesus' teaching is to hear God's word of hope for us. "I have reserved for you a future full of hope."

To allow the word of God's hope for us to soak into our bones and our brains, our depths and our depression, is to be already in the process of healing, the path of shalom. The word of God does what it says powerfully, effectively.

> For just as from the heavens,
>     the rain and snow come down
> And do not return there
>     till they have watered the earth,
>     making it fertile and fruitful....
> So shall my word be
>     that goes forth from my mouth;
> It shall not return to me void,
>     but shall do my will,
>     achieving the end for which I sent it.
> *(Isaiah 55:10-11, NAB)*

God wants to bear our burdens. God's word promises us that it will indeed accomplish just what God wants.

Not only to those gathered on a Galilee mountainside two thousand years ago, but today, to us, Jesus cries out: "Happy are you...!" Jesus intends, wills, passionately desires that we be happy. In our depression we are poor in spirit. We are the sorrowing ones, the persecuted, hungry that justice be done on our behalf, and Jesus wants us to be happy. When we hear his word, read his word, speak his word, sing his word, dance his word that word is powerful and effective. That word creates now the happiness Christ wants for us. Scripture does what it says. Christ's will prevails.

One of our colleagues, a spiritual director, tells of an

elderly man she had known for some time. One day she opened their session by noting his agitation. "Yes," he responded, "I have something very painful to ask you." She waited. "As you know, my wife is an alcoholic. I am just crushed that we will be separated for all eternity. But I wonder whether I will go to hell too because I am the one who taught her to drink...." His voice trailed off, his head was bowed.

The director pondered in her heart and responded, slowly, reverently: "Your wife is a good woman, John, with a terrible disease. You are not responsible. God wants you together, healed and happy, forever in eternity."

She was surprised—and delighted—that John believed her immediately. Reflecting on her experience, she realized that his secret fear and shame had burdened him with a kind of depression. His own relationship with God was such, however, that once he heard aloud from a Church authority the Good News of salvation he was ready, as ready as the parched earth, to soak up this word. God's plan for John and his wife is peace, not disaster, a future full of hope. For this couple, and for us, God continually lifts the heavy load from our backs and from our hearts. God bears our burdens day after day.

# Our Tear-Catching God

God is close to the brokenhearted. The word *God* is laden with so many meanings that wars have even been fought to secure one absolute meaning of that word. The word evokes many different images. For example, some Christians believe that God, instead of being close to the brokenhearted, is actually the breaker of hearts. While we all try to accept suffering, changing what we can and yet accepting what we cannot change, these Christians rejoice in suffering, framing their pain as a sign of God's love for them. And they can quote Scripture to prove their point.

Their image of God as the breaker of hearts, the breaker of spirits, however, is at odds with God imaged as one who does not crush the smoldering ember or break the bruised reed (Isaiah 42:3), symbols for our bruised and battered hearts. The biblical images do contradict one another. But the God Jesus and the prophets revealed to us is a God of love and compassion. We need to ask whether our images of God are consistent with this God of Jesus.

Another ambiguous symbol in Scripture is darkness. In our own experience of depression, darkness may be a symbol for our confusion and stumbling, the exhaustion that yearns only for sleep. Job wondered why, in his misery, he could not just be wrapped in darkness. He cries out:

> Why is light given to the toilers
> and life to the bitter in spirit?
> They wait for death and it comes not;...
> [Those] whose path is hidden from them
> and whom God has hemmed in! (*Job 3:20-21; 23*)

When the patriarch Abraham fell into a deep sleep "a deep, terrifying darkness enveloped him" (Genesis 15:12). When Moses entered into a dark cloud, however, it was there that he met his God (Exodus 20:21). As the philosopher king Solomon later noted, "God intends to live in thick darkness" (1 Kings 8:12). In the New Testament the cloud into which Jesus' three friends entered both terrified them and yielded a vision of Jesus' future glory and God's affirmation of him (Luke 9:34). Depression can transfigure our images of God and our experience of darkness. It can become a privileged place of meeting God and knowing God in darkness itself.

Images, because they involve so much of the human person, often carry more power than the concepts we may have been taught about God. In this chapter, we will explore how biblical images and our own images of God have been formed. Because images of God can both cause depression and shape how we deal with it, we need to let the Spirit of God transform these images for our healing. Realizing that Scripture offers not absolute, literal truth but the truth we need for our salvation, we can keep our eyes fixed on Jesus as the most complete and true image of God. Finally we will present three images of God that have special meaning in our suffering and depression: God as a catcher of every human tear, Jesus as the one who wipes away tears and the Spirit as our comforter.

"Those who are crushed in spirit God saves" (Psalm 34:18). So many of us are frightened of, repelled by or drawn to cheer up those who are crushed in spirit. If there is a massive denial of death in our society, as anthropologist Ernest Becker says in his Pulitzer prize-winning book, *Denial of Death*, there has been a fairly widespread denial of depression as well. Lately, however, some in our society are willing to designate depression as the common cold of emotional distress and/or mental illness.

We have already distinguished depression, a clinical condition, from the sadness that is part of the human condition. In the grip of the passion of bereavement and grief, we may feel passionately joined to God or desperately, tragically distanced from God. We may feel tenderly consoled by God or enraged at God, perhaps even hating God. In depression, however, many of us feel incapable of any passionate attachment. When we are depressed we may feel too crushed, too depleted, too exhausted to do much more than moan or whimper to God. We may doubt that God hears our whimper. We may feel nothing of God but abandonment.

One priest, like the prophet Jeremiah, reminds us to be honest in our feelings with God. This priest, while feeling abandoned and abandoning, is actually deeply engaged with God. He writes:

> I often do not want to experience God when depressed. I want to be left alone by everyone, including God. Perhaps especially God. When I'm depressed I do not want help and yet I am acutely aware that I need help. This is part of the terrible frustration and madness of being depressed. My prayer then is my anger at God, my complaint. God is present as the one I want to run from, but cannot. I talk and curse and yell endlessly at God when depressed. I am tremendously angry and fearful when depressed. It feels like there is no room for anyone else in this anger and fear. I can't maintain anyone else's presence; it's all I can do to maintain myself.

Christian spiritual traditions have named some of these feelings of abandonment, alienation from God and darkness as desert experiences. For Israel and for Jesus, the desert was a lonely, hungry time of temptation, and yet a place where God actively formed and transformed the beloved ones. The dark nights of John of the Cross, the periods of desolation described by Ignatius of Loyola, can feel much like the "pit of destruction," the "muddy swamp" of depression. In depression, however, there is none of the adventure of night or desert travel, no wisdom or warfare as in Ignatian desolation. We feel just emptiness, prostration, misery often to the point of bodily pain. The psalmists describe this helplessness and hopelessness as billows sweeping over them (see Psalms 42:8; 69:3).

God is close. In both the transitional times of spiritual dryness and desolation and in our dull depressions, God is close. In the human condition, which is always with us, and in the clinical state of depression, God is close.

## Forming Our Images of God

Most of us first came to know and love God when we were children. Even if our parents practiced no formal religion, their awe at creation, their helpless grief over sickness and death, their love, however imperfect or limited, stirred in our childish hearts a felt understanding of what we later could name as mystery, transcendence, the Other, God.

We gradually became aware of our parent(s) being in relationship to some Being called God. At age three, four, five, when we saw our parents, who towered like gods over us, on their knees in faith and worship, we began to build our image of this God of theirs. Our parents may have explicitly helped in this formation, teaching us Bible stories, prayers, family devotions. They handed on to us not so much intellectual truths and doctrines, but those images of God that shaped their own faith.

If, for example, they imaged God as a judge with a checklist, monitoring each act and secret thought, yet they themselves related with us in warm and welcoming ways, our own image of God probably tends toward the warm rather than the severe. The attitudes, affections and actions of our parents are stamped more deeply in our being than what they formally taught us.

Some of us were threatened in our preschool years with some version of: "God will get you." That image of God may terrorize us still. One man tells of hearing that warning as he, three years old, piled chair onto table, books onto chair, in order to touch the ceiling, a feat for him akin to walking in space. He toppled unhurt before he could reach his goal. As his mother wiped his tears of frustration, she reminded him: "See, God punished you for disobeying me." Well loved as the youngest in an affectionate family, he had no hesitation then in filling his squirt gun and moving through the home shooting each religious picture and statue.

Most of us would have cringed before that mother's image of a vindictive God. Many of us carry painful, terrifying images of God from these preschool years. And we pass them on even yet to our youngsters. "You'll go to your room without dinner if you don't say grace right," a father thunders at his four-year-old. In earlier days it might have been: "You'll go to hell (or to purgatory for eons) if you don't say or do or be right." The God of some adult Christians thunders still.

The God we imaged as youngsters was indeed our father and our mother. If our parents were absent (even through no fault of theirs, such as untimely death) or abandoning, alcoholic or workaholic, controlling or demanding, violent or easily manipulated, our God will probably share the same characteristics. If our parents were available and listening, encouraging us in our best dreams and desires, loving us as we were rather than as they wanted us to be, our God will continue to do likewise.

In actuality, the attitudes and actions of our parents as well as our perceptions and memories of their attitudes and actions are a mix. An accepting father has one day of rage each year; a mother who has violent outbursts becomes a tender nurse when her child is sick. No wonder our images of God can be so ambiguous and ambivalent.

## To Know the Unknowable

How, then, can we ever "know...the only true God, and the one whom [God] sent" (John 17:3)? If we turn to the Jewish Scriptures, we find violent images of God as warrior, judge, destroyer. But we also discover images of God as a rock of safety, shepherd, refreshing dew, tender mother, bearer of our burdens. Because Scripture flows from the religious experience of human beings, the images offered by Isaiah, various psalmists or the compilers of Genesis will vary.

According to Vatican II, Scripture offers us the truth that we need for our salvation (see *Dogmatic Constitution on Divine Revelation*, #11).

Which images fill our desire for God? Which images of God stir us to trust and love and worship? Those are the images that lead to our salvation. This is the truth we need. Two examples from the Jewish Scriptures may illustrate this.

First, in Exodus 3:4-14, the story of the revelation in the burning bush, Moses wanted to know God's name before he risked his life against Pharaoh. God offered Moses an event, a name and an image. From the burning bush, God pronounced: "I am who I am." The image of a fiery deity, supreme and self-sufficient, deeply impressed Moses.

Yet in Exodus, chapter 33, Moses asked to see God's beauty. The awesome transcendence came very close as God protectively placed Moses in the cleft of a rock and passed before him, crying out a new name, a new image: "The Lord, the Lord, a God of womb-compassion, slow to anger, full of kindness, and forever faithful..." (see Exodus 34:6).

God's beauty is like that of a mother whose compassion springs from her fertile, creating womb, a womb that protects and nurtures and rocks us gently. There is anger, necessary in any intimate relationship, but it is neither frequent nor excessive. God is kindness and faithfulness. Images of God for Moses, and for us, change, develop and continue to reveal the mystery of God, who is infinitely knowable.

Ezekiel the priest provides a second example. Images of God, for the Jews, were embodied quite often in the actions of God, actions always on our behalf, for our salvation. God is imaged in Ezekiel 34 as a good shepherd, gathering us all home. God speaks:

> I myself will pasture my sheep, giving them rest. The lost I will search for, those who stray I will bring back. If they are injured I will bandage them, if they are sick I will heal them, but the strong and the healthy I will _____ (see *Ezekiel 34:15-16*).

## For Reflection and Prayer

*Take a few minutes now to ponder how carefully God tends each kind of human need. However we find ourselves at any given moment—hungry, lost, hurt, frightened—God meets us as we are. No need to shape up in order to meet this God. Instead, God comes to us, takes the initiative in our healing. Which phrase in the above passage from Ezekiel best describes your feelings right now? Share that feeling with God.*

*Now notice the blank at the end of this reading. In the original manuscript, the verb, God's action, is disputed and two quite different meanings are offered. How would you fill in the blank? What does God do with the strong and the healthy? Let the first uncensored response leap out of your heart and mind. Write down that word. Look at it. Then show it to God and tell God how you feel about that word to the strong and healthy. Is that word good news? Now let God tell you how God fills in the blank. Try not to think; quiet your mind and see what bubbles up in you. Write down God's word.*

The word you chose to fill in the blank is a fairly accurate indication of your image of God. Some responses might be: God tests...God uses...God humbles...God loves...God ignores...God keeps in their place the strong and healthy. Various English translators resolved the manuscript's ambiguity with their own, perhaps unconscious, image of God. The Catholic *New American Bible* claims that God will destroy the strong and healthy. Indeed some Catholics, Presbyterians and Baptists are often taught a God like that. The older edition of the *Revised Standard Version*, an ecumenical translation, takes a middle position: God will watch over the strong and healthy. *The New English Bible*, produced by the Anglicans in Great Britain, proclaims the good news. In that translation we read that the strong and the healthy God will set out to play.

## Jesus, Our Gospel Criterion

With differing translations, differing experiences and images of God, how can we find the truth we need for our salvation? We can look to Jesus as the best image of God to see how Jesus treated the strong and healthy. "Whoever has seen me has seen the Father," he said (John 14:9). Jesus came, and still comes, not to destroy, not even merely to watch over from a distance, and certainly not to test or humiliate. Jesus comes to bring life, life in abundance. Jesus wants us to be strong and healthy. This is the good news, our gospel criterion for who God is.

As we watch Jesus in the Gospels, so attuned to peoples' suffering, we see that he also enjoyed the strong and healthy: his disciples; Martha, Mary and Lazarus; Zacchaeus, strong at least in worldly success. Jesus looked on the rich man with love, accepted Nicodemus' questions, enjoyed a wedding feast with his mother. He found strength and health in a Samaritan woman and set her out to play. She was so delighted with the fountain of living water she discovered deep within herself that she hurried to round up her neighbors to come and meet Jesus. Jesus, bringer of abundant, extravagant love, wants to set us out to play.

Jesus is the most complete image of God, the New Testament tells us. All other images of God fail. God is greater than all our images, more than we can ever say. God is more than a person, more than a force, more than an energy. God comes to us and is with us in personal ways, in energizing ways, yet God is free to be who God will be. God invites us to cling in trust, yet God will not be held or bound or defined by us. Being able to accept this paradox is a sign of our spiritual maturity.

## Shifting Images

Coming to accept the paradox of God, however, can be painful. Especially for those who cherish their relationship with God, the breakdown of former images of God can trigger depression. Images and symbols of the divine break, shatter and lie like fallen idols. Devotions, church activities, prayer, everything of God that once delighted us now dulls the human spirit. It may be that in such a process we are being "converted from our goodness," a phrase crafted by Sebastian Moore, O.S.B.

Saint Paul provides an example of this kind of conversion. He claimed that in keeping more than six hundred precepts of the Jewish Law he was perfect (Philippians 3:6). However, Paul's images of God, of morality, even his image of perfection, were shattered when he encountered the risen Christ on his way to Damascus. Imagine Paul's great disillusionment. His body expressed the trauma of this shattering in his temporary blindness. He needed new vision in order to discover a new and quite incredible image of God, God made visible in a crucified carpenter from Nazareth (Acts 9:1-19).

God invites us to let go of our old images, to trust God's new revelations to us. God also invites us to play. We can, like the Israelites, play with a variety of images of God. For example, they called God a rock, which became for them a cool shelter from the desert sun. God can also be for us the cool refreshment of ice cream sliding down our throat on a blistering hot day. God is our rock, God is ice cream. Obviously, God is neither. God is neither, but so much more. God is father, God is mother; God is neither, but so much more. For many who are depressed, God is a warm bed, God is sleep, God is the one who carries worn-out lambs.

### For Reflection and Prayer

*Take a few minutes to sit quietly, asking the Spirit to let your own images of God bubble up from deep within you. Do not censor any of them; simply see what flows. Without judging or prioritizing, jot them down. Draw them. Dance them. Cry them. There are no right or wrong images, no better or worse images. Trust the Spirit to teach you, to give you a glimpse of who God is for you, who God wants to be for you.*

As you may have discovered, all creation images God, that "Beauty ever ancient, ever new" (Saint Augustine). "The world is charged with the grandeur of God," to be sure. God, however, is also present and at work in:

- destruction ("where sin increased, grace overflowed all the more"—Romans 5:20);

- decay ("unless a grain falls to the ground and dies, it remains just a grain of wheat; but if it dies, it produces much fruit"—John 12:24);

- depression (God "is close to the brokenhearted, the crushed in spirit"—Psalm 34:19).

In our tears and terror, let us image our God as a tear-catcher. In our crushed condition, God is the one who pays attention to us. God is a minder, as the British say, a minder of frails. God is especially well imaged in the bruised body of the Crucified One.

### Jesus, the Image of God

Jesus is not only the image of God, but is completely human. He, like every human being, is made in the image of God, but in the most complete way he puts flesh on the heart of God. He is like God most fully; he is like us completely.

We have to ask: Did Jesus ever experience the terrible debilitation of depression? Jesus is like us in everything but sin. To the author of that statement in Hebrews (4:15), sin means high-handed rebellion, not weakness, sickness, failure. Jesus bore our infirmities and diseases, as the early Church proclaimed when it applied the words of Isaiah to him, especially in his final suffering. So it is possible that Jesus experienced depression. Jesus is our pioneer, according to Hebrews 12:2, our leader and the perfecter of our faith. He pioneers for us the assurance that depression, trust and hope can coexist in the same psyche.

Take, for example, Jesus' reaction of silence before his judges and torturers. For centuries we have admired his "meekness." Indeed, he may be accepting serenely what he could not change. It is possible, however, that in his powerlessness he is too drained, too hopeless, to respond. He is carried along by these final events of his life. Popular devotion pictures him stumbling, struggling, falling en route to Calvary.

Jesus certainly felt and expressed a variety and range of sadness. From the moment he was expelled from the warmth and quiet of his mother's womb, he experienced anguish, anxiety, angst. The root word for these emotional pains is *angostos*, Greek for a narrow, confined space. This claustrophobic choked feeling expresses our basic human anxiety and anguish. Jesus knew those emotions in all their paralyzing helplessness, not just on the day of his birth but throughout his life.

Jesus knew sadness born of failure and frustration; he cried over Jerusalem. He knew terror expressed in rage, exploding at his dearest friend Peter, who tried to warn him away from the danger of Jerusalem. Jesus knew deep grief; it caused him to groan and weep before his beloved Lazarus' tomb. All these feeling memories were and are yet encoded in his nerve cells: yesterday, today and forever.

Finally, the night before he died, Jesus was so terrified of death that he sweat blood. Tempted like us in every way, his good news may have tasted like ashes at that moment, his healings simply illusions. When he reached out for comfort from his three friends, he felt abandoned; when he offered himself to God, his torturers arrived. "Not my will, but yours be done," he prayed. His experience in the garden of Gethsemane has every appearance of a panic attack. What was/is God's will for Jesus? What is God's will for us?

Many of us fear God's will and try to keep God at a distance. God's coming close can frighten us. Some point out: "Look what God did to Jesus." God's will for Jesus in the garden of Gethsemane seemed to be betrayal, abandonment, arrest, torture, false witnesses, abuse of power, oppression, pain and death. Yet the Jewish Scriptures consistently portray God as hating abuse, oppression and injustice of any kind. God does indeed hate those forces that finally killed Jesus.

Jesus, too, who put flesh on the heart of God, devoted his energy to welcoming the abandoned, healing pain, preaching good news. To see Jesus is to see God in action (see John 14:9). Jesus' will for welcome and healing is God's will, what God passionately desires. God's will is welcome, freedom, truth, healing. "My plans for you are plans of peace, not disaster," God assures us (see Jeremiah 29:11).

So where is God in this most anguished time of Jesus' life, his agony, passion and death? God is definitely not, as one middle-aged Catholic suggested, the original child abuser. God did not abuse Jesus and never willed his tortured death. God did not lead Jesus to death. Being human meant that Jesus would have to die. But even in the thirteenth century the great theologian Saint Thomas Aquinas knew that Jesus' first baby breath would have saved humankind. God did not need a bloody sacrifice, and certainly did not want injustice wreaked on this good man. God never wills violence and injustice.

What Jesus needed at that moment in the garden of Gethsemane was to be true to himself. That meant being true to the good news he preached, good news about God's unconditional love and faithfulness. God's plans for Jesus were shalom—peace, wholeness and integrity. Jesus needed to die with integrity. God desired Jesus to be free, so Jesus freely lay down his life (see John 10:18) rather than deny one iota of his personal experience of God as loving, extravagantly and faithfully loving.

## The Tears of God

Where was God at Calvary? How was God faithful and loving in this event? Once we have realized that God hates the injustice perpetrated on Jesus, we can imagine tears as the most appropriate response God could have made. If Jesus wept over Jerusalem, how much more God must have wept over the crucifixion.

More and more people, it seems, taught by the Holy Spirit when they pray, are coming to know in their gut, in their heart, that God has oceans of tears. For example, one woman burst into tears in 1983 when she heard on the radio of the bombing of the United States Marine barracks in Beirut. In anger and anguish she shouted out to God, "Where are you, God?" She heard a response to her question, a voice filled with agony: "Oh, Joan, I'm crying too!" As ordinary human beings throughout the centuries have cried over Calvary, how much more God has wept. As we weep over so many injustices, evils, violent deaths in our world today, how much more does God weep?

### For Reflection and Prayer

*Pause now to let the tears of God wash over you. Remember the sorrowful mysteries in your own life. Choose only one for this exercise (tomorrow you may want to select another one). Remember this first sorrowful mystery of your life in as much detail as you can. See yourself suffering. Ask God for the gift of feeling and feel again now those former feelings, or the numbness of shock. After your memories and feelings are clear and you have claimed them, invite God to be with you. If your image of God is a personal being, touch or hold God, or let God hold you, if you can. If God is a spirit or force, let God wrap you round or stir deep within you. Now listen as God cries over your pain. God cries with you. Try to stay present to yourself and to God.*

### Jesus, the One Who Wipes Away Tears

"To see me, Philip," Jesus announced at the Last Supper, "is to have seen the Father" (see John 14:9). To know what Jesus wants is to know what God wants. Jesus wants to wipe away our tears, remove burdens from our backs, give us the peace the world cannot give, flood us with life in abundance.

If we choose any story from any of the Gospels we find

Jesus putting flesh on God's compassion and steady devotion to us. Many times in the Gospels, people sought out Jesus. At times, however, he took the initiative as "the minder of frails." The widow of Nain, for example, was one of life's frails, bereft not only of her son, but of her life support. Jesus minded her, paid attention to her grief, moved right into the funeral procession, to wipe the tears from her eyes (Luke 7:11-17).

In the same chapter of Luke's Gospel another woman was sobbing her heart out, grief stricken. She had quite a reputation in town. The men who had probably used her had only judgment for her, no tears. She produced enough tears to wash a grown man's feet, the feet of Jesus. He wiped her tears even as she wiped his feet with her hair. He was not embarrassed by this woman, but was deeply moved by the truth of her love (Luke 7:36-50).

Peter wept after he denied Jesus (Mark 14:72). Luke notes that Peter's bitter tears began to flow when Jesus turned to look at him. Peter was exposed by that look, and the exposure dredged up shame from which there was no hiding. Imagine what their reconciliation must have been like when the risen Jesus came to him on Easter night saying: "Peace be with you" (John 20:19). With just a look and those words of peace, Jesus could wipe away Peter's shame and guilt.

### For Reflection and Prayer

*Choose one of the three stories above in which Jesus wiped away tears: the widow of Nain, the unnamed woman who washed his feet, or Peter. Or look up any of your favorite stories in the Gospels. Visualize the character in as vivid detail as you can, hear the background noises, smell the scene if you can. Then notice Jesus as he moves to heal loneliness, pain, deficiency of some sort, guilt or shame.*

*Pay attention as he wipes away the Gospel person's tears. That person is you. Put yourself with your tears and your situation in that same Gospel scene. See, hear and feel Jesus relating with you.*

## Spirit-Comforter

If Jesus is God's way of being close to us, in our very flesh, then the Spirit is the risen Jesus' way of being among us, with us and deep within us. After God raised Jesus from the dead, the first community of disciples knew that the Lord Jesus was alive, present, working among them and even deep within their hearts. "[W]here the Spirit of the Lord is, there is freedom. All of us...are being transformed into the same image...such is the influence of the Lord who is Spirit" (2 Corinthians 3:17b-18).

The Lord Jesus, as he had promised, would not leave them (or us) orphaned. God would send "another Paraclete" (John 14:16). *Paraclete*, a legal term, means an advocate or attorney. Literally it is someone who calls us, someone at our side, a defense attorney. Gerard Manley Hopkins gave a sermon in the Britain of the 1890's in which he likened the Paraclete's work to that of a third base coach. Transfer his image from England's cricket to North America's baseball and picture yourself racing around the bases, head down as you barrel along, trusting the Paraclete to see the whole field, hearing the Paraclete cry, "Come on, come on! You can do it!" A guide, an encourager, a coach, the Paraclete sends you sliding into home!

*Paraclete* is commonly translated as "consoler" or "comforter." To console does not necessarily mean to cheer us but to be with us. The Spirit is with us in our loneliness. Comforting does not necessarily mean taking our suffering away but being together with us as a source of strength. The emphasis in the Spirit's consoling and comforting is on the words *together* and *with*. Truly we are never left orphans. We are being transformed, Paul writes, through the influence of the Spirit. *Influence* means a flowing into; when the Spirit of Christ flows into us there is power and energy deep within us.

The words *power* and *energy* translate the same Greek word and often are another name for the Holy Spirit. The Spirit is the power and energy of God within us. Those who are in

Twelve-Step recovery groups call on their Higher Power when overwhelmed, defeated by alcohol, drugs, gambling or other addictions. *Higher Power* translates into Greek and back again as *Deeper Energy*. For those defeated by depression, a cry to our Deeper Energy, the Spirit, who lives within us, can bring healing. Depression saps our energy, pulls the plug on our personal power. The Spirit, God's own power and energy deep within us, comforts us and energizes us as we ask, little by little, day by day.

### For Reflection and Prayer

*Imagine a large quilt, fluffy, colorful and warm. If you own such a quilt, bring it out and let your body actually feel the comforter in this exercise. Tuck the comforter around your shoulders, leaving your head free. Feel the softness, the warmth, the curl of the comforter as you rest for a while. Let the Spirit-comforter wrap you round like this, in freedom and in rest. This simple form of contemplative prayer has great power to heal.*

### The Power of Images

One of the pains of depression is the narrowing of our vision, the stifling of our imagination, the flood of darkness that blinds and confuses us. Jesuit scholar William F. Lynch writes in *Images of Hope: Imagination as Healer of the Hopeless* that the great foe of mental health and wholeness is our human tendency to absolutize. When we create and live by absolutes, he writes, we have created idols doomed to shatter. Yet when life terrifies us, we cling to our absolutes and certainties.

To absolutize means, simply, to judge in all or nothing terms, to allow little or no ambiguity in our vision of the world. The gift of our imagination can heal our absolutizing tendency. Imagination lets us play with new ideas and possibilities, lets us try on various feelings to see how they fit. We have seen in this chapter that many and varied images of God can free us from the absolute tyranny of our idol-gods: the tyrants and despots and list checkers of our childhood;

the motorcycle cop of our adolescence, hiding behind the billboard ready to swoop out to arrest our first impure thought or action; the possessive, demanding judge; the breaker of hearts and snatcher of joy whom we may have bowed before in later life.

We have the power within us to replace one image with another. We need to treat violent and despotic images of God as the impure and blasphemous thoughts they are. Should we at any point in our day find ourselves being controlled by an image of God that is not good news, we can replace it at once with the image of Jesus.

We can recall Saint Teresa's contemplation—looking at Jesus looking at us humbly and tenderly. Mark's Gospel tells us: "Jesus looked at the man tenderly" (see Mark 10:21). Because the word of God is effective, doing just what it says (Isaiah 55:10-11; Hebrews 4:12), to read that Jesus "looked tenderly" makes his affectionate gaze at us present right now in our lives.

### For Reflection and Prayer

*Hindus recite a thousand names of God; Muslims have a hundred names for God. The Jewish Scriptures and Jesus himself used various images of God, as we have seen.*

*Sit quietly and ask the Spirit to let your names for God bubble up from deep within you. Do not censor anything. Trust the Spirit to bring to your consciousness whatever names and images of God need healing.*

# 'Know That I Am God'

*Be still, and know that I am God* (see Psalm 46:10).

Some types of depression slow us to a terrifying stillness. Other types torment us with agitation and anxiety. A number of our respondents felt God tangibly present in the turbulence or in the stillness of their depression. For example, a most poignant testimony is penned by a woman who was crushed by a miscarriage:

> Sometimes I could hardly put one foot in front of the other. Everything was a huge effort. I actually could feel, physically feel, God touching my cheek to console me. A friend sent me that psalm verse about the brokenhearted, and I felt that as very validating.

Another woman shares an image of God's breaking through her depression:

> As a child I learned to use a magnifying glass to position a beam of light from the sun onto a piece of paper. The paper would eventually burn, starting very slowly, at the center, until it was gradually consumed. As I look back, I recognize God in the silent scream of rage coming from the core of my being. God was working deep within me to set me free. God, like that magnifying glass, pierced a hole through my chaos and let the smallest ray of light shine until I was consumed by this light and set on fire with love, gentleness and compassion. This took years.

A priest writes of how, locked into depression accompanied

by panic attacks, he learned who he was and who God was while attending his first AA meeting:

> Sitting in a group of men at an alcoholic rehab center, ashamed of being an alcoholic and even more ashamed because I am an alcoholic priest, I was telling my story of alcoholism for the first time. At that moment I experienced God as tremendous love and warmth, coming toward me. I was being loved simply for being honestly myself.

These three respondents claimed vivid experiences of God's presence in the depths of their depression. This is not the case, however, for everyone who is depressed. Three pastoral counselors commented on their clients' experience as they related with God in the midst of their depression. The first counselor noted that many of her depressed clients report that God seems absent, and worse, that God seems to be playing a nasty trick. The second counselor noted that God is present for many of the depressed on an intellectual level only; the heart seems to dry up. The third described her belief that God provides a kind of safe "holding environment," not necessarily felt by the client, but visible to the therapist. She writes:

> God holds the brokenhearted as does a wrapping of cellophane. God seems to be completely absent to the one experiencing depression. To me, however, God appears as a transparent sheen around the person. The broken person wonders where God is, and yet does not know that something outside of herself is holding her together and will not let her go. The observer, the one ministering to the brokenhearted, feels the pain, yet also feels and knows the presence, the sheen, engulfing the depressed one.

Those of us who have known and felt God's presence fairly steadily throughout our lives seem more severely bereft than those who only discover their spirituality in the midst of or after a depression. A middle-aged woman writes about her grief:

In my early years I truly believed and felt that God was crazy about me. I wish I could feel that security again. I've come to think that God is busy about many things and that I am not one of them. I'd like to think and feel that the Lord would leave the ninety-nine to seek for me when I'm so lost in depression, but I feel that the loss of me is just not that important.

About half our respondents experience a sense of God's absence accompanying their depression. This "loss of God" makes the absence of any other human joy or peace more bitter and severe. Some of us may even assume guilt or feel shame for "losing" God.

There surely are times in everyone's life when God seems distant, unconcerned, even powerless. One of our respondents, a middle-aged married woman, chronicles the depression and the absence of God that eventually led her out of the convent. In the midst of her darkness, she was able to image God in a new way:

> While I strongly suspect that elements of depression were present in childhood and adolescence, I think my convent years were marked by the most depression in my life. I do recall meeting God on the mountain at our motherhouse before final vows. I did have moments of "consolation," many from a book, title now forgotten, that described the presence/absence of God. Its image, "the north face of God," helped me to hang on to the idea that God had not totally abandoned me. The side of a mountain called the north face is usually the most difficult to climb: rugged, scoured by winds, snow, cold.
>
> At the end of my first year of graduate school I was quite depressed. I did some summer service at one of our convents near the water and thought about drowning myself in the harbor. I continued to experience the north face of God.
>
> Although I eventually left the sisters, although I am not now depressed, God remains somewhat distant. I see my husband's faith and wish I could have his sureness about God's goodness. Coming to

        appreciate the feminine aspects of God has been
        healing.

Sometimes we can identify what might be blocking our relationship with God. If we receive that insight, can name the block and bring the pain of it directly to God, the barriers may melt. Sometimes more is needed. A spiritual director can listen to our story of grace and stay with us when it seems the fountain of grace has run dry. A confessor can help us distinguish true guilt from the negative self-denigration that so often accompanies depression. Sometimes these helpers might suggest therapy or even medical treatment for some sources of depression, such as scrupulosity or an obsessive-compulsive disorder.

The Christian tradition often calls this sense of God's absence a desert experience or a dark night. In writings on the spiritual life, from Saint Paul's "seeing through a glass darkly," to Saint Gregory of Nyssa's approach to God in and through darkness, to the writings of Saint John of the Cross on the dark night as a lifelong process of purification, darkness has a place. From our own experience we know that the stars appear far more brilliant and numerous in the night sky when we are far from the city lights.

Teachers of prayer encourage us to persevere, even when God seems far away. *Seems* is the operative word. Believers know with an intuitive certainty that "the light shines in the darkness,/and the darkness has not overcome it" (John 1:5). For example, one ninety-three-year-old who feels that God is not present still knows—and says so with great and smiling fervor—that God dearly loves her.

Other spiritual writers insist that God does not want to keep us at a distance but wants to come close. As Saint Ignatius of Loyola phrased it, the ordinary state of the Christian is consolation. God wants us to be happy, not suffering. God passionately desires our shalom. If God is not withdrawing from us, then, especially not when we are most helpless in our depression, what is it that blocks the peace and wholeness that is God's will for us?

We have discovered at least four blocks to relationship with God and the expression of that relationship through prayer. These blocks are sin, anger with God, perfectionism and fear. These four blocks can also contribute to depression.

## Sin

Mature Christians have grown beyond merely keeping the Ten Commandments; they are beyond gross and unmistakable sin. How do we then uncover subtle sin, so uniquely personal to our situation? When we are depressed, when negative thoughts twist our self-understanding, it is usually counterproductive to "examine our conscience." Too often this is like applying a Brillo pad to an already bruised and battered heart. When we are not thinking straight, and even when we are, it is more effective to ask the Spirit of truth to reveal to us the truth of our self and our sin. Specifically in times of depression, the wise and gentle Spirit can best show us our sin.

Sin in God's eyes is not necessarily what we might call sin. Jesus spent some of his ministry trying to convert the Pharisees from their pride in their goodness. Jesus himself, like us in every way except sin, behaved in quite a few ways that the Pharisees labeled sin. For example, the Pharisees taught that a Jewish male put himself into a state of alienation from God—what we would call mortal sin—if he touched a leper, a corpse or a menstruating woman. Jesus did not hesitate to commit the "mortal sin" of touching those who were cut off.

A great gift Jesus offered his contemporaries, and offers us today, is the good news that when we sin—and we all do—we are loved. Especially when we sin we are loved. The good news is that the God of Jesus Christ loves us unconditionally. The good news is that Jesus comes for those who are sick with sin. "I did not come to call the righteous but sinners," he proclaims (Matthew 9:13). Jesus spent himself to assure sinners that God loved them with as much abandon as a father racing down the road to embrace his prodigal child (see Luke 15:11-32).

Instead of drumming people out of the community as our culture and even some of our Churches try to do, Jesus welcomes. For example, unwed teenaged mothers, gays, ex-offenders or current criminals are today's "tax collectors and prostitutes" Jesus spends so much of his energy appealing to, hoping to welcome them into the community of loved sinners. Jesus puts no conditions on their welcome. Peter shows us how the friends of Jesus can sin, and sin again, even seven times seventy times, and be forgiven.

When a real but subtle sin blocks prayer, the Spirit of Jesus is always available to teach us truth. We might begin each period of prayer with a short invocation: "Holy Spirit, teach me my sin." Within a few days or weeks, whether during prayer time or during the day, an insight or intuition will arise and we will see a new area of our sinfulness. This subtle sin is not for our rooting out or our stamping down. We need not—and perhaps should not—roll up our spiritual sleeves and get to work on it. When the Spirit leads us to new self-understanding, the Spirit can be trusted to wean us from the sin and heal us, if indeed that is what we really desire. The Spirit attends to our deepest desires.

One woman who has a devotion to the Spirit as a fountain of living water welling up deep within her (see John 7:38) realized that a huge boulder, formed by bits and pieces of sin and selfishness now grown hard, was blocking that fountain. The water of the Spirit could never be stifled, so she imaged it seeping out from under the boulder in her heart. Her energy for love and life felt blocked as well, and she truly wanted the flow and splash of the Spirit-fountain again. In times of prayer she pushed and shoved at that boulder, determined to unclog the source of living water. Failing that, she imaged laying some dynamite under it; she would break it (her sin) into pieces.

She shared this desire with her spiritual director, who asked her to invite Jesus in to size up the situation. When she did, she was amazed. Jesus walked slowly to the boulder, looked at it carefully, tenderly. He patted it and stroked it and finally put his arms around it. He was embracing her sin. She was sure it was too heavy for him and told him so. He just smiled at her and lifted the rock off the fountain's source.

## Anger Unexpressed

Another block to our relationship with God, others and life itself is anger unxpressed, and sometimes even unfelt. Tantrums, rages and obstinacy are all a normal part of negotiating in childhood. We call it "the terrible twos." Some children have anger whipped out of them at that stage. Others have their spirits broken by sarcasm and humiliation as adolescents. Girls have a cultural prohibition against expressions of anger. It seems safer to bury our anger deep within our bodies than to feel it. It does not go away, however, no matter how long it may be hidden. In fact, it may be working against us in secret, not only against our emotional health but against our physical, relational and spiritual health as well.

Anger with any authority figure could have been truly dangerous for us as youngsters. If, as adults, we have not claimed our own inner authority, we may still cringe and placate not only authorities but even peers rather than state our piece of the truth and perhaps contribute to conflict.

Anger has many sources, for example, a false sense of entitlement, fear, a desire for justice. We may dare to vent at a store clerk (a bullying sense of entitlement) or spontaneously yell at a driver who cuts us off (a release of fear) or seethe about a piece of state legislation (desire for justice). Anger with those we love, however, can frighten us deeply. Marriage counselors assure us that if there is not conflict as well as caring in a relationship, it is doomed. Lack of conflict indicates that one partner or both are negating themselves. The one who continually "gives up" in order to save a relationship eventually begins to feel helpless and victimized. The next step often leads the victim to become a persecutor, perhaps nagging or becoming passively aggressive. Straightforward communication of needs and wants, honest negotiation to reach mutual desires and decisions, what family therapist Virginia Satir termed "leveling," strengthens relationships. So do "fighting fair," acknowledging honest differences and being willing to work through conflict.

Anger in these times need not be brutal, sarcastic, explosive, icily silent or contemptuous. As we develop a sense of our true inner self, we come to view anger as a signal, as a protector when we fear that our inner boundaries are being violated. We learn to say, firmly and respectfully, "No" or "I will not stand for that." Sometimes in our anger we do fail, we abuse, we sin. Expressing anger is a risk. However, as Saint Augustine teaches: "Hope has two daughters, anger and courage." Since the gift of hope is such an antidote to depression, it behooves us to risk anger, to feel it and express it in appropriate ways.

What if our anger is with God? What if we are so angry and resentful that we even hate God? Jesuit Pierre Wolff titles his small but powerful book *May I Hate God?* Wolff's response is yes. In fact, some fruitful Christians do indeed hate God for periods of their lives. Anger is a common feeling toward God. If anger is not allowed into our consciousness when we pray, however, anger unfelt and/or unexpressed will most likely block our relationship. What is true in our human relationships usually is true in our spiritual life, our relationship with God.

A thirty-nine-year-old woman entered therapy shortly after her alcoholic mother died. She was experiencing depression for the first time in her life. Although she was not sad, she was overwhelmed in secret ways by a new lack of autonomy, feelings of confusion and general irritability, an inability to concentrate and to make decisions.

God and prayer were quite central to her life and often threaded through her therapy material. As she explored various sources of her irritability, it became clear that she had spent years hiding her anger even from herself. With her mother's death, her anger began to leak. She eventually named it and claimed it: anger with her mother, anger with her sweet but codependent father, anger with herself for modeling her own sweetness on his. She was watching her mask of kindness crack; her false self was in its death throes. Her woman therapist was puzzled, however, that this client never became angry with her or with God.

One day, after a couple of years of weekly meetings, the client suddenly realized that her therapist could die, and was in fact vulnerable at that moment to a certain disease. On learning that, the client spontaneously leaped to her feet—something totally unusual for her—stepped in front of the therapist, looked upward, raised her fist and shouted at God: "Don't you dare take this woman from me!" She sank back into her chair, utterly exhausted, and quietly said: "I think I'm finished now with therapy."

This woman had faithfully tended her relationship with God. She thought that she had learned in a long Ignatian retreat that she was a creature and not God. However, she quite unconsciously felt entitled to special treatment from God because of her religious devotion. Her mother's death had violated her sense of justice. How dare God take her mother? She had been furious with God and did not know it. When she felt her anger in the therapy session and expressed it, she was flooded both with relief and with a kind of humility. Once again she had come to know in her gut that God was God and she was not God. As she interpreted the incident in the therapist's office, the right relationship between God and herself was restored because she had dared to be her true self, her enraged and wounded self, with God.

## Perfectionism

It is obvious in the Gospels that the scribes and Pharisees were good people. Paul, a Pharisee, claimed that in keeping the Law he was perfect (Philippians 3:6). For these Jews, God's own self was expressed through the gift of the Torah, the Law. Pharisees honored God's self-expression with perfect obedience. As we know only too painfully from our own experience, anything, even God's own self-expression, that becomes too central in our life can block God.

Using religious language, we call such a narrowing of focus idolatry, having a strange god. Law, even God's Law, can become such an idol. Scripture or religion or any particular devotion can become an idol. So can our striving for perfection. In psychological language we would call this narrowing of focus absolutizing. Jesus pointed out this absolutizing tendency to the Jewish leaders when he said to them: "You search the scriptures, because you think you have eternal life through them;.... But you do not want to come to me to have life" (John 5:39-40).

Jesus came "so that they might have life and have it more abundantly" (John 10:10) and they missed him. Their focus on the Law was too narrow. They missed God's expression in the fullness of time, Jesus himself. Instead of the author of life, they preferred perfection.

One line from Matthew's Gospel seems to have tortured many Christians who are sensitive to God's ways. Jesus said: "So be perfect, just as your heavenly Father is perfect" (5:48). Striving to be perfect, striving to be God, is doomed to failure. It is also the source of much depression. Perfection has many meanings. In the family it might mean keeping all the rules, bringing home good grades, never fumbling the football on the two-yard line, stifling anger or tears or exuberance. One of our clients testified that in her family, "Boys will be boys and girls will be perfect." Perfection in school looks like straight lines of little children, never chewing gum or whispering, but with hands folded on top of the desk, two feet on the floor. Perfection in Church means attending Mass, obeying God's laws, never sinning, maybe even never really enjoying oneself. Even when the parent, teacher or pastor has never, and would never, voice such high standards, children strive to please.

It is dangerous when we begin to fault ourselves for not being perfect, for not being God. Some of us fall into a sinkhole of depression when our ideal self shatters, whether by true sin or by the emergence at last of our true but flawed self. What may look like sin could well be grace abounding, the grace of being set free like Saint Paul from the shackles of perfectionism (Romans 5:20-21).

In our struggle to be perfect, instead of keeping our eyes fixed on Jesus, we keep our eyes fastened securely on ourselves and our spiritual progress in perfection. We might translate perfection as the Roman ideal of moderation in all things or the Stoic ideal of being without passion. Our English word *apathy* stems from that Stoic ideal. We Christians in our drive for perfection can look like people who have no life, let alone life in abundance (John 10:10). This apathy and perfectionism can lead to an inability to feel, which is a symptom of depression, not holiness. While apathy may accompany depression, deliberately to crush our passion, our deep and lasting emotion, can and does bring on depression.

Paul, converted from his perfectionism and energized by his passion for Christ and the Good News, proclaimed the passionate God of the Jews. But the culture in which he proclaimed the gospel was so influenced by Stoic philosophy that for almost two thousand years the official spirituality of many Christians has been influenced by the Stoic ideal of apathy. When these Christians hear "Be perfect," they translate it to "Be without passion, be apathetic, be controlled."

In the original Greek of Matthew's Gospel, the word *perfect* means "headed toward the goal." Of course the goal is God. To be headed toward God is Matthew's meaning for perfection. Luke simply changes the word in his Gospel, where Jesus says: "Be compassionate just as your Father is compassionate" (6:36, *New Jerusalem Bible*). Jesus invites us to deep and powerful passion with our God.

Sharing passion, sharing our deepest feelings and desires with someone, leads to and deepens and nourishes intimacy in human relationships. Perfectionism only skews human relationships; it does the same in our relationship with God. Sharing passion and being compassionate strengthens human relationships and bonds us with God.

## Fear

If we were to read straight through the Gospels of Mark, Matthew or Luke, we would be struck by how frequently Jesus reassured those who were distressed by saying, "Do not be afraid." A particularly helpful translation is: "Fear is useless. What is needed is trust" (Mark 5:36, *NAB* 1970). How could Jesus have preached what he himself had not experienced? Like us in all his emotions, he must have wrestled with the various everyday fears that pepper our lives. He felt his fears and shared them with God; the outcome was a deepening of his trust. Out of this experience, he could assure people then and now: "Do not be afraid. Trust."

Fear can block any relationship: for example, fear of intimacy, fear of a particular race or gender, fear of commitment, fear of failing, fear of rejection. It is not surprising, then, that many people report that fear blocks their relationship with God. A certain fear is appropriate when we approach the creator and sustainer of the universe. This fear is awe, a kind of worship. Without an element of that awe, we might trivialize God. For all that Jesus invites us to a trusting, childlike intimacy with a loving God, Jesus never spoke of God as just "one of the boys," a good pal with whom to shoot the breeze. Intimacy, whether with friends or with God, is meant to increase our reverence, not dilute it.

Some of us who are afraid of intimacy with human beings learn first how to be intimate with God. Our relationship with God eventually turns us outward in gradual trust and growing friendship with others. Others of us first learn, often through trial and error, friendship with another person, and that prepares us to know and love God more intimately.

We will list some of the fears in relating with God which those who pray faithfully have named. Although we will try to defuse them rationally, we know that it is God who teaches truth and we believe deeply that God's truth will gradually set us free from our fears.

**Fear of Being Known.** Some people are frightened by the

thought that God knows them so thoroughly, without their knowledge and consent. This feels like a violation of personal boundaries, an invasion of privacy, a trampling of God's own gift of personal freedom. The antidote seems to be to level with God, to tell God just what is comfortable for us to share. We trust that God, unlike some parents, will not intrude; unlike some spouses, God will not try to read our minds. If we reverence God, how much more God must reverence us.

**Fear of What God Might Ask Me to Do.** If we ask God to do something for us, it is fair that God may ask us to do something in return. The key word is *ask*. Asking presupposes that both parties are free to say no. Some people never feel intimacy with God or with their friends until they do say no. We risk conflict. When we say no to God (and we are not speaking of gross sin), we can learn how seriously God takes our freedom. Unlike some parents, God does not punish us for asserting ourselves. We are free to say no. We are free to say later. Saint Augustine prayed: "Make me chaste, Lord, but not yet." There is no shame in gradual growth.

**Fear of Being Found Wanting.** God is not content to give us just what we need; God wants to lavish on us all that God is (see Romans 8:32). Our lack allows God to give and give and give, grace upon grace upon grace, as John's Gospel puts it (see John 1:16).

**Fear of Being Unworthy and Thus Shamed.** If shame means an emptiness at the core of our being, for whom better to hold our gaping hole open? We do not need to make ourselves worthy. That is the good news that Saint Paul discovered in his conversion. To try to make ourselves worthy of God would exhaust us and prove futile. The good news is that God, and only God, makes us worthy.

Poisonous shame derives from our being shamed and humiliated when we were too young to ascertain the truth of matters for ourselves. Inappropriate and toxic feelings of shame can themselves be a source of depression. If our thinking is not crooked, when shame rises in us now, we can determine whether it is an appropriate emotion. God does not humiliate us. Proper feelings of shame alert us when we are pretending to be God. When we try to control, when we usurp the freedom of others, and these manipulations are discovered, shame is an appropriate emotion.

**Fear of Failure.** To fail in a relationship with God is fairly difficult. It takes two to make a relationship and our Partner is supremely committed. Even when we feel that we are failing and falling, we have the certainty that Christ has hold of us. "I stretch forward," Saint Paul writes, "to take hold of him who has already grasped hold of me" (see Philippians 3:12).

**Fear of Freedom From the Law.** To be free, to be responsible, can be frightening. We sometimes like to have definite boundaries and let someone else be responsible for our behavior. When we grow in intimacy with God, however, consciousness of Law diminishes and eventually disappears. As Saint Paul writes in his Letter to the Galatians (see 3:19—4:11), when we are immature in the faith, we need the Law of God as a tutor. Law is like a guide and guardian for a child, making the child feel secure within the boundaries of the Law. As we mature, Paul writes, we no longer live by Law but in the freedom of the Spirit. Without Law, we may feel insecure at first. Without Law we can no longer take our spiritual pulse, no longer tick off all the rules we have kept. Merit and earning our rewards from God dissolves into the grateful realization that we are entitled to nothing. God is generous, as we see in the parable of the vineyard workers called to work at different times of the day (Matthew 20:1-16). Instead of hoarding our merits and wages, we can become available to all that God wants to lavish on us.

**Fear of Giving up Sin.** Closeness with God will wean us from sin. The operative word is *wean*. When a baby is ready to give up the breast or the bottle, it happens. God is not brutal in stripping us of sin. Yet as we come to know God more deeply and become more and more fascinated by God's goodness, subtle sin gradually loses its allure.

**Fear of Being Healed.** Intimacy with God will eventually heal us. That will mean, perhaps, a change in life-style, a change of friends, a change of self-image. When the paralyzed man was healed by Jesus, he could no longer be tended by family and friends; he had to take responsibility for himself, he had to work for a living. Perhaps the loss of a former identity as the sick one, the depressed one, the unloved one, the adult child of an alcoholic, will cause some grief.

When Saint Paul lists the last fruit of the Spirit (Galatians 5:22) as "self-control" he means the work of the Spirit in our lives that leads us to take responsibility for ourselves. This kind of responsible self-acceptance that healing brings is not a virtue to strive for but the Spirit's gift. Self-control is a fruit that the Spirit plants, tends and grows within us.

**Fear of Letting Go of Illusions and Control.** To move into God is to move into permanent insecurity—but what an adventure. When the Spirit of truth teaches us, illusions crumple. Some of our most precious illusions are about God, about Church, about ourselves. When they disappear, we can feel adrift, alienated, until new understandings, more tentative, more humble truths replace them. Some of us, in our illusions, even try to control God. For example, we may insist that God who is present and active in all our daily activities show up in a blaze of glory during our time of prayer. Or we may try to bribe God by fasting. God is utterly free.

**Fear of the Unknown Abyss.** Some of us are afraid that union with God means total absorption of our whole person into God. God does not engulf us. As in any healthy union, loving ever more deeply paradoxically deepens the distinctiveness between the two persons. The distinction is that God is God and we are not God. The *Catechism of the Catholic Church* (#2670) reminds us that we are in the process of becoming divine: "If the Spirit should not be worshiped, how can he [sic] divinize me through Baptism?" (Gregory of Nazianzus). "...[W]e are God's children now," the First Letter of John exults; "what we shall be has not yet been revealed. We do know that when it is revealed we shall be like [God]" (3:2). Yet we are distinct, not God. We are the beloved of God.

## Our Pioneer in Relationship

As any good preacher will, Jesus must have preached from his own experience. At the end of his life he knew excruciating fear in the face of death, but fear may have haunted him all his life. When he preached about trusting the God who clothes the lilies, would he not have had to be tempted, like us, to that mistrust which is born of fear?

Like us in everything, he enjoyed and wants us to enjoy an intimate relationship with God. He is our pioneer, blazing a trail through whatever blocks we may discover in that relationship. He embraces the boulders and the blocks, and especially accepts and embraces our depression. Those who are crushed in spirit, whether through sin, anger, fear or perfectionism, are the very ones for whom he yearns.

# Why?

Our Jewish ancestors in the faith were not sunny sufferers. We think of the psalms as songs of praise, but most of the one hundred and fifty psalms are laced with the cries of the brokenhearted. Within the Book of Psalms are various literary forms including hymns of praise and thanksgiving as well as the groaning, moaning psalms called laments. Jesus' own prayer would have been steeped in the laments. Let us examine this type of prayer, the lament, so prevalent in Israel.

## The Laments of Israel

Our English word *lament* comes from the Hebrew word *lamah*. *Lamah* is a cry of grief, a question hurled at God: Why? The Israelites, as Moses was quick to notice, were a group of grumblers. Never satisfied, they complained against their leaders and against God. "[T]he Israelites murmured there and tested the LORD, saying, 'Is the LORD in our midst or not?'" (Exodus 17:7). God nevertheless cherished them.

The people of Israel ritualized their groaning in the lament, a prayer form found most frequently in the psalms, Isaiah and Jeremiah. An entire book of the Jewish Scriptures is named Lamentations. Laments include curses and begging as well as questioning and complaining. Sometimes laments are songs of repentance and then thanksgiving for God's mercy. Some of these songs offer powerful, accurate and many-faceted descriptions of depression.

In the laments we can recognize the bodily repercussions of depression: the faint spirit, the inarticulate sleeplessness, aching bones and parched throat.

I cry aloud to God,
   cry to God to hear me.
On the day of my distress I seek the LORD;
   by night my hands are raised unceasingly;
   I refuse to be consoled.
When I think of God, I groan;
   as I ponder, my spirit grows faint.
My eyes cannot close in sleep;
   I am troubled and cannot speak. *(Psalm 77:2-5)*

I am weary with crying out;
   my throat is parched. *(Psalm 69:4)*

My strength fails in affliction,
   my bones are consumed. *(Psalm 31:11)*

...my bones burn away as in a furnace.
I am withered, dried up like grass,
too wasted to eat my food.
From my loud groaning,
I am become just skin and bone. *(Psalm 102:4-6)*

### For Reflection and Prayer

*The Israelites believed that when they remembered an action of God
their remembering made the action present again here and now.
Look again at the psalm verses above. As you read these psalms, try
to pray them. If memories flood you or trickle in as you pray, stay
with the memory from your own life. Perhaps a word or the feelings
or an image from the psalm will touch your heart. Stay with them
as long as they move your heart. Reading these psalms and
remembering your own life is a form of prayer.*

Psalm 22, which begins with that haunting cry of
abandonment, "My God, my God, why have you abandoned
me?" vividly depicts not only the emotional but the physical
ravages of depression:

   Like water my life drains away;

all my bones grow soft.
My heart has become like wax,
 it melts away within me.
As dry as a potsherd is my throat;
 my tongue sticks to my palate.... *(Psalm 22:15-16)*

Laments often include a sense of alienation and/or isolation:

I am like a desert owl,
 like an owl among the ruins.
I lie awake and moan,
 like a lone sparrow on the roof. *(Psalm 102:7-8)*

From the ends of the earth I call;
 my heart grows faint. *(Psalm 61:3)*

Especially painful is the sense of being lost, confused, forgotten by God:

My tears have been my food day and night...
I say to God, "My Rock,
 why do you forget me?" *(Psalm 42:4, 10)*

How long, LORD? Will you utterly forget me?
 How long will you hide your face from me?
How long must I carry sorrow in my heart,
 grief in my being day after day? *(Psalm 13:1-2)*

Powerlessness is a theme in the laments. It is vividly described:

The breakers of death surged round about me;
 menacing floods terrified me.
The chains of the underworld enmeshed me;
 the snares of death lay in wait for me. *(Psalm 18:5-6)*

This helplessness seems, and may indeed be, pervasive for years:

My life is worn out by sorrow,
 my years by sighing.
My strength fails in affliction,
 my bones are consumed. *(Psalm 31:11)*

Depression can feel like slip-sliding into death:

> Save me, God,
> for the waters have reached my neck. *(Psalm 69:2)*

> My days are like a lengthening shadow; I wither like
> the grass. *(Psalm 102:12)*

The psalmists describe these feelings to God, directly addressing complaints to the One who may be imaged as a disciplinarian, tester and punisher in one breath; and a savior and vindicator of the suffering in the next.

Sometimes the psalmists blame God for this wasting away. They do not hesitate to question God's intimate involvement in every moment of their days and nights, every movement of their hearts. Like us, they seek a cause for every effect, and God must be that cause.

We believe that God in Jesus heals rather than hurts. Yet when we are afflicted with tragedy we may want to blame God. Our intelligence assures us that God does not want innocent suffering, that God does not test a family with untimely death, that God does not punish a nation with a typhoon. Yet the most human response to tragedy is to cry, Why? Whom better to cry to than the One who bears our burdens day after day (see Psalm 68:19)?

God does not cause, does not even permit these tragedies. Instead, God waits with us in hospital rooms, stands in the breadline among the hungry, cries with those made homeless by earthquake. God is neither testing us nor punishing us.

God does not permit pain, which can be as cruel as causing it. The image of God that this "permissive will" evokes is one of a distant potentate, arms crossed before him, watching us squirm. Classical theologians could write of the four wills of God, one of which permitted suffering. This assumes that God causes everything and has a patriarchal power over everything. Power like this controls all, fixes all, rescues all. We once believed that this was God's style of power, but the definition of power as control and our belief in that patriarchal worldview is now being questioned.

God continues to reveal another kind of power, one we know from our own experience. This power stays with us and gives us courage. It does not rescue us from pain or pluck us out of danger, but abides with, comforts and strengthens us in our suffering. It does not hold back the forces of nature by magic, but brings new life out of natural destruction. So much of human destruction flows from the abuse of free will, and yet God's power does not interfere with human freedom. This is a different way to understand God's power. Because Jesus came to reveal that God is with us (Emmanuel) we know that this is a valid gospel understanding.

### For Reflection and Prayer

*Think for a moment of the last time you were in distress or pain. Remember one specific incident in detail. Where were you? What was the suffering? Was anyone with you or did anyone come to you? Who? What specifically did that person do? Was it a comfort to you? What was that person's power in the situation?*

We have used the above exercise in a number of workshops. Participants most often describe the person who comes to them in their distress as simply being there, staying with them, often not even talking. What the person did for them they describe in various ways. Sometimes the one who was with them listened, affirmed, held, accepted without judgment or moralizing. The participants recognized the power in the encounter. It is a simple step to conclude that if human beings can effect this kind of power in one another's lives, God can even more be with, stay with, listen, affirm, hold and accept. When we asked the participants, "Did you want the person to fix the situation for you?" quite often they seemed puzzled. "No, the person was a great comfort just sitting with me, supporting me," they usually respond.

To understand God's power in this way we may have to give up our expectations of a rescuing and fixing God. Twelve-Step programs teach us that "expectations are planned resentments." We may harbor some resentments against God for failing us in our expectations of rescue. This is a kind of theological crooked thinking. Those resentments may lie deep within, repressed and depressing us. The Spirit challenges these expectations. It is such comfort to have a friend stay with us, simply be with us, without expectations of rescue, problem solving or fixing. God offers to stay with us always. The celebration of Jesus as Emmanuel, God-with-us, cannot be confined to the Christmas season, because his power effects healing day by day.

## Cursing Psalms

The psalmists did not merely groan to God about the hardships of life. When they were the victims of others' cruelty, they laid their desire for revenge before God. They cursed. They rid their minds, hearts and bodies of bitterness through their cursing psalms. They entrusted all their negative energy to God. The cursing psalms are prayers, a form of the lament.

Although cursing psalms are usually removed from public liturgical prayers in our Churches today, let us make a case for their use. First, we must realize that with God there are no wrong or bad or sinful emotions. To feel is not to sin. To act in ways that destroy love is to sin. As God created us, we are capable of every emotion, including hatred, jealousy, despair and desire for revenge. As God created us, we are good. Cursing psalms offer us the opportunity to express these usually painful emotions to God in our prayer.

> Violence and hatred of enemies, fury and desire for vindication, are all important aspects of being human. To deny these emotions is to repress a part of our wholesome self. Repressing them insures that these same emotions will find means for asserting themselves in covert, twisted ways. (Rea McDonnell, *When God Comes Close*, p. 86)

Repressing these emotions, perhaps because they were once labeled sinful or negative, can lead to depression. The defense mechanisms we often use to hide away the shame of these emotions is called denial. It buries our true feelings, especially those that are often painful, deep out of sight. If we find it difficult even to feel these emotions, we surely don't talk about them readily. We fear them rather than trusting them. Israel, on the other hand, brought these feelings into the light, especially into God's healing light. Who better to receive our shouts of rage and helplessness than our God? Who better to receive our bitter tears?

God does trust these emotions or they would not have been given us. They are signals to us that we have been hurt, that our boundaries have been violated, that our self, God's creation, God's work of art, has been damaged. If we did not feel physical pain, we could bleed to death or ignore serious injury. Physical pain alerts us so that we can find proper help. Emotional pain signals us that we need God's healing presence and power.

Cursing psalms can also carry us out of ourselves to pray with and on behalf of all those suffering oppression, those too hopeless to pray for themselves. This is our prophetic call as Church. Joining with the whole Church around the world, we lift our prayer against those battering their wives or betraying their husbands, against those greedy nations and tyrannical governments, against injustices in our town or our parish.

> The sick, the hungry, the frightened in the crowded huts of the poor can be strengthened by our prayer.... [F]or them and with them, we call out curses on their oppressors to a listening God. (McDonnell, *When God Comes Close*, p. 88)

Rather than let their rage and violent feelings turn in upon themselves, draining their bodies and embittering their spirits, Israel's psalmists discharged their personal fury in prayer:

> May my enemy's days be few;
>     may another take his office.
> May his children be fatherless,
>     his wife a widow.

May his children be vagrant beggars...
May strangers plunder all he earns
May no one treat him kindly or pity his fatherless
    children....

May cursing clothe him like a robe;
    may it enter his belly like water,
    seep into his bones like oil.

I am sorely in need.
    my heart is pierced within me...
Like a lengthening shadow I near my end,
    all but swept away like the locust.
My knees totter from fasting,
    my flesh has wasted away.

Though they curse, may you bless;
    shame my foes, that your servant may rejoice.
*(Psalm 109:8-12, 18, 21-24, 28)*

National enemies such as Babylon, which destroyed Israel's temple in Jerusalem, are cursed:

Happy those who seize your children
    and smash them against a rock. *(Psalm 137:9)*

May God rain burning coals upon [my enemies];
    cast them into the grave never more to rise.
*(Psalm 140:11)*

Notice how the following psalm details each of the psalmist's pains to God. Often the curse is a call to God to double back the enemies' evil upon their own heads:

I looked for compassion, but there was none,
    for comforters, but found none.
Instead they put gall in my food,
    for my thirst they gave me vinegar.
Make their own table a snare for them,
    a trap for their friends.
Make their eyes so dim they cannot see;
    keep their backs ever feeble....

Pour out your wrath upon them;
    let the fury of your anger overtake them....
Strike them from the book of the living;
    do not count them among the just!
*(Psalm 69:21b-25; 29)*

## For Reflection and Prayer

*Try to pray the following psalm against your own enemy, whether interior, personal or political. Pay attention to how you feel. Then stop and tell God in your own words how you feel. Continue with the psalm if and when you can.*

    *This exercise may release deep emotion in you, especially if you are not used to being angry in prayer or in life. Share your emotions with God, knowing that they are God's good gift to you. Let us pray:*

*Oppose, LORD, those who oppose me;*

(Name those people, those forces)

    *rise up in my defense.*

(Tell God what protection you need)

*Make their way slippery and dark...*
*Let ruin overtake them unawares;...*
    *let the snares they have set catch them;*
    *let them fall into the pit they have dug....*
*Clothe with shame and disgrace*
    *those who lord it over me...*
*Then my tongue shall recount your justice,*
    *declare your praise, all the day long.*
(Psalm 35:1a, 2a, 6a, 8, 26b, 28)

We have just prayed that God do justice for us. Many of us have been fearful of God's justice. We may think of justice as our society has too often defined it. Our country practices violent revenge against criminals and calls that justice. Not so in Israel. The justice of God means the holiness of God. Justice and holiness are the same word in Hebrew and in Greek, the biblical languages. We can throw ourselves on the justice of God at all times. In times of deep depression especially, we can count on God's justice to be much more kind to us than our own attempts to be merciful to ourselves.

## Begging Psalms

> Listen, God, to my prayer;
> do not hide from my pleading;
> hear me and give answer.
> I rock with grief; I groan.... *(Psalm 55:2-3)*

Our society ignores or reviles beggars. We do not like to ask for anything: directions on the road, medicine from a doctor, help on a project. We'd rather do it ourselves.

No wonder when we're socked senseless by the onslaught of a major depression, or even frayed around the edges, many of us find asking for an understanding ear, antidepressant medication or therapy a shame-filled experience. We try to slog through the muddy swamp all on our own. Sometimes in families, to "spare" the others, the depressed mother will take to her bedroom, the depressed father will disappear into work. Children can usually mask depression by staring, unseeing, for hours at TV. We are trained and shamed so that we do not easily ask for help.

Perhaps we have even been taught that petition is the lowest form of prayer. Adoration and thanksgiving are the ideal prayer, we suppose. Yet why did the inspiring Spirit insure that so much flat-out, desperate begging got included in the canon of our Scriptures? Even Jesus, according to the Letter to the Hebrews, spends his risen life making intercession for us. Intercession, petition, begging are beautiful and productive prayers.

Israel begs for freedom from slavery, for forgiveness for their idolatry, for water and abundant crops in the promised land. Women plead as passionately as men for fruitfulness. Hannah, for example, laments her barrenness forcefully. In her bitterness, Hannah prays, sobbing. The priest who overhears her thinks that she is drunk, but Hannah responds "I have had neither wine nor liquor; I was only pouring out my troubles to the LORD" (1 Samuel 1:15).

After Hannah had asserted herself and her right to address God in her grief, "[s]he went to her quarters, ate and drank with her husband, and no longer appeared downcast" (1 Samuel 1:10, 18). The son soon conceived was Israel's prophet-judge, Samuel.

When we examine the pleadings in the psalms, we discover the deepest desires of the human heart. Through their complaining and cursing, the psalmists hunger at a deeper level for wholeness. Sometimes they pray, "longing to see God's face," or "thirsting for the Lord." They beg for God's own self, for healing, for freedom, for inner peace. All these petitions, all this desire can be summed up in the Hebrew word *shalom*. The psalmists want shalom.

The prophets, too, long for God's shalom. Jeremiah, the most melancholic, victimized and depressed of them all, hands on to us the good news he hears God proclaim:

> My plans for you are plans of peace and not disaster. I have reserved for you a future full of hope.
> (*Jeremiah 29:11*)

To want shalom is to cry for freedom. Shalom gives us hope in our pit of anguish and anxiety. God responds: "I will restore you to health;/ of your wounds I will heal you.... I will restore [your] tents.... City shall be rebuilt upon hill" (Jeremiah 30:17, 18).

We who hate even to ask for help and healing may have to learn to beg. When we want to deny or pretend that we are not really creatures but God, then begging can be the antidote. In fact, we are creatures, created, made—and more, made from dirt. We are contingent, dependent (literally, hanging) on others. We are mortal, which means that we are oriented to the ultimate powerlessness of death. Finally, we are human, *humus*, of the earth, the dirt. An unhealthy denial of our creaturehood cries out for the deepest healing of all.

The Spirit who leads to all truth will teach us the truth of ourselves, which will set us free. At times that teaching is gradual, slow, quiet, daily, with many mediators of the truth: friends, spouse, therapist, enemies, events. Sometimes through our hitting bottom in addiction, illness or failure the Spirit teaches us more dramatically that we are not God, not the center of the universe. At the moment when we feel so flattened or shattered or ground down, simply powerless, God responds to us:

> But now, thus says the LORD,
> who created you...and formed you;
> Fear not, for I have redeemed you;
> I have called you by name: you are mine.
> When you pass through the water, I will be with you;
> in the rivers you shall not drown.
> When you walk through fire, you shall not be burned.
> For I am the LORD, your God...your savior.
> ...Because you are precious in my eyes
> and glorious, and because I love you, ...
> Fear not, for I am with you... *(Isaiah 43:1-5)*.

> I hold you and no one can snatch you from my hand.
> *(Isaiah 43:12)*

Admitting powerlessness is as old as the Jewish Scriptures. In the New Testament as well, Paul experienced that in his weakness, God is strong. Ignatius of Loyola taught the principle and foundation of all spiritual life is that God is God and we are not God; we are creatures. Millions of recovering addicts, working the first of the Twelve Steps, continually admit their powerlessness. Once that basic truth of our dependent creaturehood has been established; once we realize that we can count on God, not on ourselves, for freedom, fullness of life and shalom; once we know in our gut and accept that we so desperately need God, then we have peace. Acceptance of our one and only self leads to peace. Even in the midst of illness or failure or shame, we rest in that peace of God that surpasses all we could ever hope for or even imagine.

In depression, healing happens partly because we

acknowledge the truth of our humanness. In depression we do beg. We plead, pray, cry, groan, lament. We are like Israel. In all their responses to trouble and tragedy, Israel prayed. To *pray* in the Hebrew language is simply to ask. And asking, in the graphic scenario set around many Hebrew verbs, means to stroke the face of God.

### For Reflection and Prayer

*Open your Bible to the Book of Psalms. Choose any psalm and begin to read it slowly, noticing what the psalmist is begging for from God. If it is a prayer for something you need/want, pray it again in your own name. If the plea does not resonate with your needs right now, choose another psalm.*

*After you have found a psalm that expresses your begging and have prayed it as your own, choose just one line from the psalm and use it throughout the day as an anchor. You might imagine yourself approaching the smiling face of God, lifting your hand and stroking God's cheek. Sleep disturbance is often a symptom of depression. If that is true for you, you might image your pillow as the chest or the lap of God. As you long for sleep, imagine God stroking your face.*

## Psalms of Repentance

Admitting sin is often as difficult as admitting powerlessness in today's society. A deep sense of unworthiness, shame, lies at the core of many of us. We can deny and mask shame in so many different ways. One way is the frantic attempt to prove ourselves worthy: worthy of love, worthy of power, worthy of recognition, worthy especially of God. We find it so difficult to take in the good news that God has already counted us worthy, even when we felt and feel: "But I am a worm, hardly human,/ scorned by everyone, despised by the people" (Psalm 22:7).

When there is emptiness at the core, at the heart of our being, we may try to stuff the hole in our heart. Friends, food, work, sex, religious devotions can at best offer temporary relief. Is there anyone among us who at some time in life did not try to fill the gaping chasm of unworthiness with good works? We kept the rules of family, laws of country, commandments of Church and often went the extra mile in our deeds of charity. Yet we remain plagued by the continuing, gnawing shame that we are not good enough for God. Or, on the other hand, why the parading of our perfection, trumpeting to call attention to our charitable works? Sometimes it is when we feel most hollow that we almost compulsively try harder. Jesus' parable of the Pharisee who marched to the front to "pray," but instead detailed his works of piety (Luke 18:9-14) punctures the hollow emptiness of the Pharisee's boast.

The parable continues with the description of the tax collector who prayed, "Lord, be merciful to me, a sinner." This is the cry of the person who knows a deep need for God. God does better than mercy. God becomes compassionate, sharing the passion, the feeling, with us. As the man in the parable goes home, justified, so we are healed by our admission and God's compassion.

"Lord, be merciful to me, a sinner" is a common refrain through many of Israel's laments. "...I disown what I have said,/ and repent in dust and ashes," Job announces after his fierce assurance of his innocence before God crumbles (Job 42:6). To repent means to change perspective, attitudes, literally to change one's mind (*meta* [change] *noia* [mind] in Greek). God longs for our repentance, as Jeremiah records:

> Return, rebel Israel, says the LORD,
>   I will not remain angry with you,
> For I am merciful, says the LORD,
>   I will not continue my wrath forever.
> Only know your guilt:
>   how you rebelled against the LORD, your God,
> how you ran hither and yon to strangers...
>   and would not listen to my voice....
> Why do these people rebel
>   with obstinate resistance?
> Why do they cling to deceptive idols,
>   refuse to turn back?

I listen closely:
    They speak what is not true.
No one repents,... saying: What have I done?
    *(Jeremiah 3:12-13; 8:5-6, NAB)*

Unlike many of us who are too fearful to cry, "What have I done?" the psalmists groan in their shame and guilt. They turn to the healer of hearts. For example, from the greatest of the penitential psalms:

Have mercy on me, God, in your goodness;...
For I know my offense;
    my sin is always before me...
Turn away your face from my sins;
    blot out all my guilt. *(Psalm 51:1, 5, 11, NAB)*

The author of this psalm is deep in the depression born of true guilt. The psalm is ascribed to King David; to cover up his adultery with his general's wife, he sent the general to the front lines to be killed in a covert murder. Terrible injustice is involved in this deed. Only by acknowledging the truth of his sin and begging God's forgiveness can David find peace and eventually even joy:

A clean heart create for me, God;
    renew in me a steadfast spirit.
Do not drive me from your presence,
    nor take from me your holy spirit.
Restore my joy in your salvation;
    sustain in me a willing spirit. *(Psalm 51:12-14, NAB)*

Depression can trap us in a corrosive feeling of unworthiness and deficiency at the core of our being (shame). Depression can magnify our awareness of a particular, actual sin (guilt). Depression can keep our eyes firmly fixed on the mud of our own making. The psalmists and prophets of Israel suggest a remedy. The experience of true, not toxic, shame and guilt springs from an acceptance of God's unconditional love and faithfulness.

God first loves us. Unconditionally, abundantly, extravagantly, God loves us. Israel understood its first covenant with God, made on Mount Sinai, as conditional: If you do thus, I will do thus. The later covenant that God makes with King David *after* his grievous sin is unconditional. In the time of the new and final covenant, Jesus gives us images that express God's unconditional and extravagant love. Think, for example, of the abundant joy of the woman who finds her lost coin and the extravagant banquet of the father who welcomes home the prodigal (Luke 15). These are Jesus' images of God.

God wraps us round in mercy, compassion, tenderness and kindness. In Hebrew, those words for God's love are often linked with words for God's faithfulness, God's steady, consistent, devoted fidelity, lasting forever, never shaken through all generations.

When we have accepted God's faithful, steady love and unconditional acceptance of us, then we can dare to face and admit our real sin. Real sin produces true, not neurotic, guilt. Real sin is revealed to us, most often quietly and gently, in the light of God's already having loved and accepted us. Real sin may have little to do with our notions of law, morality and failure. There is no need to scrape ourselves raw with spiritual Brillo pads. True sin comes to light through the kindly teaching of the Spirit of truth. The response to this revelation of our sin is not depression but gratitude for having been loved so well into the light of truth.

Toxic shame needs healing. God never humiliates or shames us. Our feelings of deficiency and unworthiness are transformed instead in the steady kindness of God's acceptance of us, just as we are. True shame, like all emotions, is God's gift to us, a signal. True shame is our acknowledgment that another is God, and God-for-us.

## Lamenting in Nazareth

Israel's laments—complaints and curses, pleading and penitence—came to fullness in the prayer of Jesus. He would have learned to lament in his home, as a child of Israel. If we read the beginning of Matthew's Gospel (1:18-25), we can only imagine how Mary may have lamented her pregnancy of unknown origin. In that Gospel, only Joseph learns what is happening to his betrothed. In Luke's Gospel (1:26-38), on the other hand, Mary receives the message from the angel. How might Joseph have lamented?

### For Reflection and Prayer

*In your imagination, take the part of either Mary or Joseph as they face this crisis. Try to get inside their skin and feel their feelings. What would Mary have felt if, as in Matthew's account, she had no clue as to how this pregnancy happened? How will she speak to her parents? What will she say to Joseph? Most importantly, how will she pray? What can she say to God in her confusion, fear, agony?*

*What would Joseph have felt if, as in Luke's Gospel, he had no message from the angel as he slept? When Mary tells him she is carrying a child, out of wedlock, how does he cope? How does he share his fear, anger and sense of betrayal with God? How does he lament?*

The Law insisted that Joseph have Mary put to death, stoned, burned or drowned for her presumed adultery. What groans to God must have poured from his heart. There was pain on both sides, misunderstanding, such a broken trust in this budding relationship. Their suffering surely cried out to God.

Joseph, being a just man, a man truly close to God rather than rigidly close to the Law, decided against capital punishment for Mary. Joseph had already made this decision not to avenge his honor through capital punishment; only then did the angel reassure him.

According to Luke's Gospel (2:1-7), how the young couple must have lamented the cold, jostling trip to a strange city for a census decreed by an oppressive government. Would Joseph have lamented his powerlessness to provide shelter for Mary at her time of delivery? Would Mary have lamented over being attended by a husband who, as a carpenter, was probably not familiar with live birth? Would she have cried to God, "Why can't my mother be here with me now?"

Israel's laments always end with thanksgiving. Within the lament is embedded trust, thanks for God's comfort and hope for future blessing. Blessing for the future, Jesus himself, has come in the flesh.

# The Laments of Jesus

In this chapter we will focus on Jesus' laments and on our own laments, the loud cries of the Body of Christ today. As a youngster and young man, Jesus would have deeply immersed himself in the prayer life of his people. Keenly aware of foreign oppressors in their land, Jews of his time would have complained loudly to God about their national problems. Jesus too would have laid all his feelings, both personal and political, before God. He would have asked, Why? He would have cursed, begged and even repented; his attitudes would have undergone metanoia. In baring his heart to God he would have discovered a release of bitterness and a flooding of his being with trust, thanks and hope.

When his friend Lazarus died Jesus wept and groaned deeply (John 11:33, 35, 38). The inarticulate cry of anguish would have been directed, wordlessly, to God. Jesus began to pray his trust aloud: "Father, I thank you for hearing me" (John 11:41). Only then did he cry out in a loud voice, "Lazarus, come out!" (John 11:43).

Jesus also sobbed over Jerusalem (Luke 19:41-42). He may have felt so discouraged that he considered throwing himself down the cliff. While of course there is no scriptural evidence for such desperate thoughts, if he was tempted like us in all things, why not this most frightening of all temptations? What if his feelings of hopelessness tempted him to consider the possibility of suicide? When he was tempted, he prayed. He not only addressed God but the city in this lament: "If today you only knew where to find shalom...."

How many other situations would have stirred Jesus' sorrow, frustration, rage? What other daily setbacks would have led him to bring his broken heart to God in prayer? When he went to the mountain to pray alone, did he cry, sob, curse? He could have emptied his fury at the Pharisees into a cursing psalm. Then collapsing in exhaustion he would have waited for God's comfort, encouragement and peace to fill him. Those who are crushed in spirit, God saves (see Psalm 34:18).

## A Possible Incident

Jesus cursed a fig tree when he was hungry because the tree was not bearing fruit (Mark 11:12-14). Peter pointed out to Jesus that the tree was withered to the root (Mark 11:20-21). Perhaps he was remembering a time when Jesus had withered him. Jesus had warned his friends that, contrary to their expectations of a powerful messiah, he would only find suffering, rejection and death. "He spoke this openly. Then Peter took him aside and began to rebuke him.... [Jesus] rebuked Peter and said, 'Get behind me, Satan'" (Mark 8:32-33a).

By calling Peter Satan, Jesus was basically calling him damned, damnable, a messenger of darkness, a father of lies. What could have been happening in Jesus to have brought him to this fearsome and furious outburst? Jesus, like us in every way, was not eager to suffer rejection, torture and death. To speak about it openly must have left him feeling quite vulnerable.

Peter stepped in to argue him out of it, and Jesus probably felt threatened. Intuition, the prompting of the Spirit deep within him, led him to imagine his death with some accuracy and with great dread. As with many of us when we feel threatened, we lash out at those closest to us. Was Peter withered to the root? Was Jesus?

What happened next? Mark's next mention of Peter indicates that six days later Jesus took Peter, James and John with him to the mountain of transfiguration (Mark 9:2). During those intervening days, how might Jesus' prayer lead to a reconciliation with Peter?

## For Reflection and Prayer

*Imagine Peter getting behind Jesus, moving far behind into a clump of trees along the road. Slumping against a tree trunk, Peter sits dejected on the ground. He may have begun to pray, perhaps telling God that Jesus is not fair, not to be trusted. He complains that Jesus has time for all the nobodies and not nearly enough time for him.*

*Take it from there. You too have many complaints against Jesus. Speak them to God right now. Feel your hurt and disappointment with Jesus and his treatment and/or neglect of you. Write those grievances against Jesus.*

We continue with our story of a crisis in Jesus' relationship with Peter. As Peter literally got behind him, Jesus seemed only vaguely aware that Peter had disappeared. Jesus ended his preaching for the day. "Let's eat," he said, but his friends noticed that his heart was not in it. "I'll make a fire," Andrew offered. Eleven of them busied themselves with setting up camp for the night, and Jesus wandered forward along the road. Ahead of him loomed Mount Tabor. The majesty of the sunset coloring the mountain moved his heart to praise and thanksgiving. But he choked on his psalm of praise, coughing hard. He was alone, frightened. "Oh, God!"—almost a cry, a sob. "Hear me, my God. Listen to my cry for help!"

Suddenly tears washed Jesus' dusty cheeks. His coughs turned to gulps as he began to cry. He prayed through his tears, begging for courage, longing for Peter's presence and—whoops! He'd lost track of Peter. Jesus began to pray in words from Psalm 130, a penitential psalm:

> Out of the depths I cry to you, my God.
> If you kept track of my failures, who could stand?
> But with you is forgiveness.
> I trust in you, for you are kindness
> And you will save me from all my sins.

Jesus' breathing fell into a deep, normal rhythm. His rage at Peter must have choked him. He imaged his friend, frightened. Moved with compassion and sorrow, he prayed Psalm 51:

> Have mercy on me, God, in your goodness;
>> in your abundant compassion blot out my offense...
> For I know my offense...
> My sacrifice, God, is a broken spirit;
>> God, do not spurn a broken, humbled heart.

As Jesus prayed Psalm 55 aloud along the side of the road, he rocked back and forth, begging:

> Listen, God, to my prayer;
>> do not hide from my pleading;
>> hear me and give answer.
> I rock with grief; I groan....

Jesus now called on the power of his imagination. He imaged God smiling on Peter, embracing Peter, calming his fears, wiping away Peter's tears of hurt and rage. God, like a mother with an abundant bosom, opened the other arm to Jesus, beckoning him near. Jesus, in his imagination, looked at Peter's tear-streaked face, his pleading eyes. Oh, to be gathered with his dear companion, lost in the bosom of God, together. Jesus raced toward the welcoming arm of God. Then he was ready to put his image into action.

Racing down the road, past the disciples' camp and fire, Jesus called out for Peter. The moon had not yet risen. From the deepest dark of the small forest, Peter moved tentatively toward the road, toward Jesus....

### For Reflection and Prayer

*From the deepest dark place within yourself, listen to Jesus call your name, hunting for you eagerly. You clutch your list of grievances. Do you want to forgive him yet? Do you need to talk some things through with him in the dark? How close will you let him come? Speak with him honestly.*

## Jesus' Last Laments

Finally, we turn to Jesus' last laments. He had set his face toward Jerusalem when he told a parable of praying always, without becoming weary.

> There was a judge in a certain town who neither feared God nor respected any human being. And a widow in that town used to come to him and say, "Render a just decision for me against my adversary." For a long time the judge was unwilling, but eventually he thought, "...because this widow keeps bothering me I shall give a just decision for her lest she finally come and strike me." *(Luke 18:1-6)*

Jesus imaged God as a weary widow, crying out for justice. God laments the injustice of powerful people. God prays, begging human beings for justice, and will not give up. In one of the most cruel and unjust events in human history, God was the chief mourner. In the events of Jesus' final hours God laments.

We have no eyewitnesses of what happened to Jesus emotionally in the garden of Gethsemane. Yet each Gospel and the Letter to the Hebrews wants to record this critical moment; it contains a key truth for our salvation.

John's Gospel places the crucial event not in the privacy of a darkened garden but a bit earlier, and in public. Jesus proclaims: "The hour has come for the Son of Man to be glorified.... I am troubled now. Yet what shall I say? 'Father, save me from this hour'? But it was for this purpose that I came to this hour" (John 12:23, 27).

How deeply disturbed Jesus is! We see from this that God wanted to feel the faint heart, parched throat and burning bones, not only of physical pain but of the most profound emotional distress.

We are familiar with the Gospel scenes of Jesus' agony in the garden. Matthew, Luke and especially Mark portray Jesus' anguish and loneliness. Another author in the New Testament describes Jesus' interior struggle in the garden of Gethsemane most graphically: "In the days when he was in the flesh,

[Jesus] offered prayers and supplications with loud cries and tears, to the one who was able to save him from death, and he was heard because of his reverence" (Hebrews 5:7).

The author of Hebrews proclaims the paradoxical good news that, with loud cries and tears, weak like us, tempted like us, Jesus has compassion for and with us. He pioneers for us the path through death to abundant life.

The Greek word we translate as "loud cries" can mean the scream of a trapped wild animal. A friend on retreat told of an experience that made this expression very real. On the retreat center's grounds was a pond. The man was enjoying a stroll at sunset when a shriek pierced the dusk's quiet. Investigating the cry, he discovered at the edge of the pond a large snake in the process of swallowing a frog whole. In its trapped terror that frog screamed an unforgettably piercing shriek.

Jesus can sympathize with our weakness (Hebrews 4:15). Like so many of us, feeling trapped in depression, Jesus has descended into the pit of destruction, his own muddy swamp. He screamed in his panic and hatred of dying. The author of Hebrews insists that Jesus is like us in everything, our pioneer into death as well as in life. He has blazed a trail for us through the muddy swamp of terror and grief. In the midst of his screams he begged God to save him.

The Letter to the Hebrews tells us Jesus was heard because of his obedience (see Hebrews 5:7), his obedience to reality. Jesus' agony, betrayal, torture and crucifixion were not God's will for Jesus. All that pain, however, was the outcome of preaching the good news and healing those broken in body and spirit. That was his reality.

Many of us have equated obedience with conformity to law, God's Law. But obedience originally means "hearing." Jesus' loud cries were heard because he himself heard and responded to the cries of the poor and the outcast. He heard the wail of widows. He paid attention to women. He minded the frails of his society. He listened to God's word and the promptings of God's Spirit within him. Obedient to his own developing sense of integrity as he grew in wisdom and grace, he was heard and saved, set free, by God.

Jesus' tears were heard. He would cry *Lamah?*—Why?—during the hours of his final suffering. His lamentations were accepted by God. Why? pounded through Jesus' pain-wracked body and crushed spirit as he cried loudly from the cross in Aramaic: *"Eloi, Eloi, lema sabachthani?"* (Mark 15:34). This question—"My God, my God, why (*lema*) have you forsaken me?"—are the last words of Jesus that Mark records. Then "Jesus gave a loud cry and breathed his last" (Mark 15:37).

Volumes have been written about this final wail of Jesus before the ultimate suffering and separation of death. Some religious commentators, by spiritualizing this cry, weaken Jesus' identification with the tortured of this world. The most common comment, which also strips Jesus of his crushed humanity, is that Jesus was simply praying, using the opening verse of Psalm 22 as we might, on our deathbed, recite a familiar prayer formula such as the Lord's Prayer.

If that were true, then Jesus could also have called out in perfect trust the opening lines from Psalm 23: "The Lord is my shepherd." What is the truth needed here for our salvation? Why would Mark and the early Church community that handed on these first traditions of Jesus' dying have included such searing words?

Jesus, like us in every way, was tempted as we are to despair, tempted not to trust, perhaps even unable to feel trust. Thus, continues the author of Hebrews, Jesus is able to sympathize with our weakness, with all we face and feel. When tempted to lose hope in life, to lose trust in God, Jesus took his pain and fear and despair directly to God. He prayed: "My God, my God!"

Jesus did not hide away his despair, did not play stoic or macho, did not worry that God would not approve such weakness. When we call out to God in direct address we are not actually despairing, no matter how we feel. In real despair we would deliberately refuse to cling to God. No matter how sunk in hopelessness we may feel, God's name anchors us: "My God, my God!"

"Why?" was Jesus' next word. *Lamah? Lema?* Jesus was heard because of his obedience. Children always ask, Why? In decades past our constant "Why?" to our parents, teachers and others may have triggered a bored, indifferent or even angry response. "Because I said so" quickly taught us not to question, but to obey "blindly."

Jesus did not exhibit such an unintelligent obedience. He questioned the doctors of the Law in the Temple as a young man. He challenged the scribes, Pharisees and priests throughout his public ministry. God has gifted us, too, with questions so that, like Jesus, we might grow in wisdom. God intends us to question life, meaning, suffering, death and even God's own will, ways and self.

Did God abandon Jesus on the cross? Jesus seemed to get no response to his desperate "why." With no rescue in sight Jesus must have felt abandoned. Yet at that lowest point God was actually setting Jesus free in the open.

Many recovering addicts experience "hitting bottom." In their most profound anguish of shame, guilt and isolation they suddenly discover the freeing love of a power higher than themselves. In this ultimate depletion on the cross Jesus suddenly knew the higher power or deeper energy that propelled him through death into resurrected life. He was saved, set free in the open, heard by God in his anguished questioning, his "why."

This is surely truth needed for our salvation. *Salvation* comes from a Latin word that means health and wholeness, like the Hebrew *shalom*. Wholeness, as we have seen, is God's passionate desire not only for Israel and Jesus, but also for us. To become healthy and whole involves accepting the reality of our bodies with their range and depth of emotion. To be obedient to reality first means listening to our own bodies. When Jesus on the cross paid attention to the pain of his body/spirit, he did not deny, nor could he numb, the emotion of despair. In offering himself to God, Jesus made sure that he offered his whole self—not just his courage and compassion, but also his weakness and depression and despair.

How was Jesus heard? How was he saved from the pit and

from death itself? God did not pluck Jesus from the pit of his prison. Prisons at that time were literally deep, dark holes in the ground; the prisoner was thus forced always to stand upright. Imagine the pain, the sleeplessness of that position, akin to what some of us feel in the prison of depression.

*Save* in Hebrew means not rescue but being set free in the open, taken from Israel's primary experience of being saved from slavery in Egypt. At the time of their passing over into freedom, the Israelites were given room, space, the whole Sinai peninsula; they were given time, forty years. Their experience of salvation was being set free in the open.

Jesus passed through the narrows of terror and death as well, passed over into freedom of the risen life, transcending space and time. It seemed that death had swallowed Jesus. But he was thrust through that choked and narrow space, death, into new and risen life. He was not rescued from death, but saved from death. He was set free in the open. He lives forever. God saved Jesus, and Jesus in turn saves us and sets us free.

Jesus was and still is in solidarity with us. As Matthew wrote, envisioning Jesus as Isaiah's Suffering Servant: "He took away our infirmities,/and bore our diseases" (Matthew 8:17; cf. Isaiah 53:4). God wants the whole of us, healthy and diseased, just the way we are, just the way we feel.

# Letting God Minister to Us

God passionately desires our healing and peace. In this chapter we offer some exercises for deepening our relationship with God through prayer. We will pray for healing as we come to know and respond at a deeper level to our tear-catching God; to Jesus, the wiper of tears; to our Spirit-comforter.

The word of God is alive and heals. To read and digest God's word is to let what we read and pray happen to us. For example, if we read John 9, where Jesus gives sight to the man born blind, in our reading and absorbing the words of that long-ago event, God's word effects a healing of whatever is blind in us.

Because we are embodied people, we will begin not with Scripture but with exercises for body prayer—grounding, breathing deeply, receiving, even taking a shower. Some people find it helpful to tape-record these exercises so they can pray them without having to juggle the book.

Then we will turn to Scripture. We invite you to ask the Gospel characters you will meet in these pages to become prayer partners with you. These men and women, so many of them unnamed, lived the original events with which we—and countless Christians before us—have prayed.

Scripture accomplishes that for which God sends it (see Isaiah 55:10-11). God intends our salvation (our being set free) and our shalom (peace, wholeness, integrity). These interactions with Jesus are happening to us, for us, with us, within us right now. We are the ones discovering in his presence and activity the freedom, healing and peace we need today.

Our brains and nerve cells in and of themselves cannot distinguish whether what we are experiencing is happening in reality or in our imaginations. When we enter the Gospel story with our imagination, with both mind and emotions, our bodies register that the event has happened to us. The event, and our feelings surrounding the event, are coded in our neurons, even if the event happened two thousand years ago. Our bodies then join with our faith to assure us that events meant for our salvation are happening for us today. Ignatius of Loyola called this kind of prayer contemplation— Teresa of Avila's looking at Jesus looking at us, humbly and tenderly.

We offer both the bodily exercises and the scriptural exercises with total conviction that Jesus, very much alive, acts today on our behalf. Our faithful and compassionate High Priest lives to make intercession for us, and prays with us now.

## Bodily Exercises

**Grounding.** Sometimes emotional pain can make us feel lightheaded, mentally and emotionally scattered. This exercise reminds us that we are continually pulled toward the center—the center of ourselves and the center of the earth— by the Holy Spirit. We don't have to do anything. We can rest and let the Spirit do the work, drawing us to the center.

Sit up straight with your feet on the floor. Let your hands lie loosely in your lap. Breathe deeply, with your eyes closed.

Picture yourself melting, collapsing into your legs, your feet. Your whole self is slowly, gently sinking through the rug, the floor, the cement, to the soft, rich soil hidden beneath your house. You are being drawn through the soil, through bedrock to the center of the earth. Fire burns here at the center.

Image this fire, this energy at the center of our planet. This fire is eons old and is not consumed. Image this fire as God's own energy, the Holy Spirit. Watch it roil and boil and leap. It fascinates you, this inner energy of God and of the world. Keep breathing deeply as you watch.

The fire of the Spirit approaches you. Do you want the Spirit to energize you? You will not be burned or consumed. Trust the Spirit as the fire from the center pushes, not like a volcano, but as a gentle flame, through your feet and legs and torso. Feel the flame of God's love welling up within you, surrounding your heart. It cauterizes your open wounds, bringing healing to your pain.

Picture this flame enveloping your heart and then moving up slowly to your head. Your face is becoming radiant. The psalmist calls to you: "Look to God that you may be radiant with joy" (Psalm 34:6).

Now the flame leaps to your mind, your brain, your memory and imagination. All is drenched in the fire of God's love: your thinking and feeling, your memories and images are transformed like gold in the fire. The Spirit is transforming you.

> ...where the Spirit of the Lord is, there is freedom. All
> of us...are being transformed into the same image
> from glory to glory, such is the influence of the Lord
> who is the Spirit. (2 Corinthians 3:17-18)

As you continue to breathe deeply, in and out, let the throbbing rhythm of the flame cushion you, cradle you. You and the Spirit are so deeply united that you are becoming God's flame of love for your family, your friends, your co-workers, all whom you meet. Stay with this experience for as long as it continues to nourish you.

**Breathing.** This is an exercise for breathing out negativity. Sit up straight, two feet on the floor, so that your chest cavity is open, not scrunched as we sometimes hold it when we are afraid or sad. Picture your body as transparent. See the veins and arteries, the interior organs, your heart and lungs and digestive system. Picture bright red blood coursing through your body, bathing each and every cell with nutrients and fresh oxygen. The wastes flow out of each and every cell and a darker, bluish blood carries away the poisons.

Thoughts, memories, images and every feeling—all are gifts of God to us. Because of pain in our earlier life, however, some of these have become harmful, filled with negative energy, twisted or stamped-down energy. This exercise calls to the Spirit to wash through us, to flow through us as the breath of God. One of the earliest scriptural images of the Spirit is the breath of God hovering over the waters of chaos. Out of chaos that Spirit has created everything good. Image the healing, creative Spirit as both the breath entering your body and the air that surrounds you.

Take a deep breath and slowly expel it. Inhale deeply and slowly exhale. Breathe out today's worries. Take your time, recalling each worry. Each time you exhale, let that worry go, spilling into the waiting atmosphere of the Holy Spirit who surrounds you.

Take the frustrations of today, or this week. Slowly exhale each one as you remember it, turning it over, into the air, into the breath of God that enfolds you.

Now breathe in deeply. Breathe in the peace of the Spirit. Image that peace flooding your lungs, your heart, racing through your bloodstream to engulf and wash through each and every cell of your body. The peace of the Spirit flows through your brain with its thoughts and memories, images, feelings and desires. This peace gently but thoroughly pushes out the pain, the negative energy, the fears that cling to you.

Breathe out. Breathe out pain. Breathe in peace. Breathe out old hurts and resentments. Breathe in peace. Breathe out fear. Breathe in the love of God, the Holy Spirit. The Holy Spirit, Saint Paul writes, is the love of God poured into our hearts. Let the love of God flood your being. Continue this deep breathing for as long as it nourishes you.

**Moving.** Walking and swimming are two rhythmic activities that provide an atmosphere for prayer as well as flush our systems of unused adrenaline and lactic acid and enhance our heart and lung capabilities. Walking is a simple, safe exercise; it costs nothing. Listening to music, particularly religious music, on headphones is an obvious way to pray while you walk. Listening to the sounds of a city street or a woodland path, conscious of each foot's movement, can also be an exercise in wonder and gratitude. We can compose our own rhythmic mantra, repeated with each footstep, such as: "Jesus" or "Only goodness and love will follow me" (Psalm 23).

Swimming takes more skill and preparation, and often involves a fee. Being engulfed in the waters of pool, lake or ocean, however, provides a womb-like atmosphere of safety and comfort. To float and be carried by the water is a bodily act of trust. It is easy to image ourselves floating in the womb-waters of God's compassion. Another association might be to remember that baptism means being plunged, immersed, not only in water but in Christ Jesus. When swimming laps, we can offer each lap for some loved one, picturing the person surrounded with us in God's compassion.

**Softening.** This exercise calls for a shower. Read through the exercise; listen, imagine, picture, feel the water on your skin. Image the steps in this exercise as vividly as you can so that your whole body remembers it the next time you shower. Every day the psalmist reminds you: "Oh, that today you would hear [God's] voice:/Do not harden your hearts..." (Psalm 95:7d-8d).

Hear the water rushing from your shower. Feel the warmth, as hot as you can stand it. Smell your favorite soap. Turn your face up to the spout and taste the water. Let the water soothe your closed eyes for a moment. Now imagine the water washing away your worries, your tiredness, your discouragement, sloughing them off and down the drain. Imagine the water softening the callouses on your skin and the scabs on your heart, relaxing any hardness in your heart. It can penetrate the armor that defends you and soften you deep within. "My heart is thirsting for God like a parched, dried up land" (Psalm 63:2c). Let your skin drink thirstily as God's grace showers you. Let God's grace melt you.

**Receiving.** For those who find it almost impossible to receive, let alone beg, healing can happen as we try to "act as if," try to trust and receive, no matter how we are feeling. Again, using our bodies will imprint the exercise in our nerve cells. Sit with your hand turned up and open on your lap.

Even if you have to force yourself into this position, your memory will think it is the real thing.

We can carry this prayer attitude of receiving from God into the day. As we try less to grasp and control, to let go of our fear that we will be abandoned and forgotten unless we get it all set up, we can use our bodies to express our prayer. We need no words for this prayer. The gesture itself, in silence, is the prayer.

Whenever you catch yourself sitting with your hands in your lap, turn them over, open, a gesture of receptivity. During times set aside for prayer you might sit with open hands and add an upturned, open mouth, like a baby bird dependent on its mother. Position your self with hands and mouth open as you listen to God's yearning to lavish love on you:

> Oh my dear one, how I wish you would listen to me...
> I brought you into freedom...
> If only you would open your mouth, I would gladly
>    feed you.
> How I wish you would pay attention to me...
> I would feed you with the finest wheat, and fill you
>    with honey from the rock.
> (from *Psalm 81*)

**Bubbling Up.** Throughout this book we have suggested letting prayer bubble up in our spirits. Such prayers can be used to heal heart-hurt; they are especially helpful when our prayer life feels dry and desert-like. John's Gospel promises us that the water of life will well up deep within us. On the last day of a festival with rituals of light and water, Jesus cried out: "Let everyone who thirsts come to me and drink. I will give them a fountain of living water welling up deep within" (John 7:37-38).

In prayer we can call on the Spirit, that fountain of living water within us, to let bubble to our awareness what we need to know; to bubble from our hearts whom and how to love; to bubble up the wisdom needed for our decisions; to bubble up energy.

Set aside five minutes of quiet. Image yourself sinking

deeply into the center of your being. See and hear the fountain of water that is the Spirit living within you. Pray a simple sentence such as: "Holy Spirit, show me my gifts" or "Fountain of life, what shall I do in this situation?" or "Holy Spirit, I feel so dry."

Then wait in silence until something—or many things— bubble up. It may help to write them down afterward, but do not try to control this fountain by thinking. This wisdom is deeper than our thought.

**Bathed in Light.** The light of Christ is a healing force. We remind ourselves: "In your light, O God, we are bathed in light" (see Psalm 36:10). Imagine the Risen Christ coming toward you. His whole being is full of light, and yet he looks like—and is—a real person. As he holds both his hands out to you, you notice the light intensifying and pouring out of them. You look more closely and see the wounds in his hands. His wounds are the source of his healing light. Hear him ask you if you would like to be bathed in his light. Respond to him.

If you told Christ you were not ready for his touch, don't worry. He will not leave you. Looking at you humbly and tenderly, he will stand with hands stretched out to you for years if necessary. He respects your freedom and your readiness.

If you told him you want to be bathed in his light, watch him turn his hands over and lay them gently on the top of your head. Feel the light drenching you, not only your head, but all that your head holds: your thoughts, judgments, images, intuitions, feelings, desires, memories of what has happened to you in the past and the decisions you yourself have made. His light bathes your mind.

Now his hands move to cover your eyes. His light is healing all that you have seen that has hurt you. His hands cover your ears. The harsh and damaging words that have stuck in your ears are washed away as he bathes your ears in light. His fingers touch your lips and every harsh and damaging word you have spoken is forgiven.

Take your time with this exercise, staying as long as you

want with each movement of Jesus' hands. Be as specific as possible in your memories. If you become too overwhelmed, stop. Retreat to your safe place, or share your experience with a friend. Come back to this exercise only when you choose. Remember, Jesus will wait, ready to go at your pace.

Now Jesus rests his wounded hands on your shoulders. What burdens will he find there? Let him take the burdens from you and feel his light penetrating the soreness of your neck and the stiffness of your shoulders.

Next, Jesus kneels in front of you and takes your feet in his hands. He wants to remove your shoes and socks, but he needs your consent. He wants to wash your feet, not with mere water but with the light of his love. Look at him looking up at you, as he kneels before you. He is looking at you humbly and tenderly, waiting to see whether you will let him wash your feet. He learned at the Last Supper that his washing feet can be troublesome to some people. Will you let him bathe your feet in light? When you are finished with this exercise, be sure to rest a while.

## Scriptural Exercises

**Feeling Helpless.** A man paralyzed by weakness lies helpless at the pool of Beth-zatha (John 5:1-9). Thirty-eight years— what must it have been like for that man, waiting, unable to move for such a long time? Some of us who have spent years paralyzed by chronic, low-grade depression know this experience. Can you identify with that man?

Jesus seems to know that the man had been there a while. What clue might there have been in the man's grooming, in his facial expression? How does that man look?

Spend a few minutes deliberately tightening your body, all your muscles, but especially your facial muscles. Feel the shriveled ache of lying in one position. Bed sores? Flies? Smell? Who is this man? Does he have a family, friends, a name? All we know is the length of his weakness and the frame of his mind.

Jesus asks: "Do you want me to make you whole?"

Jesus is direct, but the man is not. He replies: "Sir, I have no one to put me in the pool."

How is he feeling? Discouraged? Cynical? Afraid of becoming whole? Afraid that Jesus is toying with him? Angry with God? Is this a whine or a simple statement of his narrowed reality that healing can only happen one way, via the pool.

Look at Jesus looking at this man, humbly and tenderly. Jesus squats down beside the man's mat so that he can look directly at him and can hear clearly whatever the man might say, even his complaints, his anger. There is so much noise in this busy place. Jesus has to listen closely so he doesn't miss a thing, even a nasty "Harrumph!"

"Do you want to be whole?" Jesus asks again.

Depression can make us nasty. It twists our thinking and our feelings. It paralyzes us, robs us of the will and energy to live. Now look at Jesus as he squats down next to you so he can listen carefully to your pain, all your pain, even nastiness. What do you see in his eyes? Now he asks you directly, using your name: "_____, do you want to be whole?"

How will you respond to him? What will you say? There is no right answer. Jesus did not turn on his heel to march away from the complaint of the paralyzed man. He will accept your response, in words, in gestures, in silence cold or peaceful. He will wait.

He says to you: "_____, stand up, take up your mat and walk."

How do you respond? Whatever your response, it is prayer.

**Feeling Hopeless.** Sometimes when we are overwhelmed with feelings of hopelessness and despair, we need to rely on the prayer of the community to bring us to God. Alone we are helpless.

In Mark 2:1-12 we hear the story of another paralyzed person. The room where Jesus is speaking is so crowded that the friends of the person who is paralyzed can't get the stretcher through the door to Jesus. They clamber up onto the roof and remove some tiles. Hear the clatter as one falls to the ground, startling Jesus who, of course, looks up. Imagine his amazement as he watches the stretcher swing and sway, and his concern as he catches the eyes of the person strapped to it. The stretcher is gently lowered before him. With whom in this scene do you identify?

If you identify with the paralyzed person, rest a moment in the realization of all the people around the world who at this minute are praying for those in pain, are praying for you. You find yourself in front of Jesus, brought there by friends and family. Let yourself experience the compassionate gaze of Jesus and bask in the warmth of all those who are praying for you. You may have neither the energy nor the will to say anything, but words are not expected from you. Silence, too, is a response. Let others hold you today.

Or you may be one of the stretcher-bearing friends. You are beside yourself with worry for a spouse, a grandchild, a friend. You are frightened that your loved one's hopelessness will never lift. You are frightened about where feelings of despair might lead. Today you are invited to be hope for the person you love. Think of other people who can help you carry this stretcher. These may be family or friends who can and will and do pray with you. They may be your own family saints, those who have gone before you and who care intensely for you. Feel your frustration with this burden. By the time you have pried the tiles off the roof and have lowered the stretcher you are exhausted, trembling, sweating, maybe even swearing. Jesus looks up through the roof at you. What do you see? He quietly thanks you and motions to one of his friends to get you a cup of water. Relax with that. Savor your water. Rest hopefully now that your loved one is in his hands.

**Feeling Anxious**. Sometimes depression is accompanied by fear, anxiety and obsessive worrying. Especially tormenting are those early morning hours before the break of day, or sleepless hours late at night. When depression makes the night endless and terrifying, God can seem far away and callously indifferent to our plight.

If this is your situation, spend some time with Jesus on the

Sea of Galilee (Mark 4:35-41). A storm rises, mirroring the tossing and buffeting that has taken place within you on waves of anxiety, fear or guilt. You think your ship is going down. A lot of good it does to have Jesus over there, asleep in the stern. It is all well and good that he is so exhausted that he is able to sleep! In a storm! You tug at his cloak, trying to wake him up. This is not fair! .

"Jesus! Jesus! For God's sake—for my sake—wake up!" You are frantic with fear; your voice tightens and rises, shrill. Your anger at his indifference, your envy that he can sleep and especially your utter fear make you shake and punch his shoulder as you shout. What do you want to say to him? Say it, directly. How does he respond?

Let him command the storm inside of you: "Be still." Breathe deeply and image the storm in your heart gradually subsiding. Rest.

**Feeling Shame.** Although we have already used Luke's story of the woman bent over for eighteen years earlier in this book, we believe that the living word meets us fresh each time we become involved in a gospel event. We will flesh out the story with what might have happened, because Luke offers only a shorthand account (Luke 13:10-17).

Jesus had set his face toward Jerusalem weeks ago. The crowds following him were increasing day by day. So was the pressure. Longing for solitude, he needed perspective. Most especially, he needed to feel loved. Often he would head out at night to pray. Alone.

He also found rest and love in the home of his friends Martha, Lazarus and Mary. The towers of Jerusalem were visible from the hillside of Bethany. While he was staying there, he hoped for some quiet conversation with the local rabbi.

The Sabbath was a raw and rainy day. Lazarus, appointed to read at the service, had left early for the synagogue. Martha refused to go to the synagogue, saying that the president was unfriendly to women. Mary and Jesus hurried along; Jesus tried to cover her head with his large cloak. They shook the rain off inside the door, and Jesus folded his cape.

"I'll sit back here with you, Mary," he offered.

She blushed. "That's not appropriate, Jesus. You can't sit with the women."

"One of my criticisms of the synagogue is this dividing the men from the women, sticking the women at the back. I'll sit in back."

"Please don't, Jesus," she pleaded. He didn't want to hear so he turned away from her, letting his gaze roam through the women's section as the service began. He watched a few latecomers shake the rain from their garments before joining the community.

A woman appeared in the doorway. She was so bent she could hardly remove her outer cape. Lopsided, she shook it off her shoulders onto the muddied ground inside the door. He reached for her cloak, shook it, brushed it, smiled, ready to hand it to her. She could not see his smile. Her eyes could see only to his knees. He squatted down so as to catch her eye, but she closed both eyes, tightened her face and turned scarlet.

This blush was different from Mary's. Mary wanted things proper, and Jesus was so outrageous that he often caused her embarrassment. This woman's blush was from shame, the shame of being noticed. The rabbis taught that physical disability was a sign of God's disfavor, usually a punishment for personal sin. Being bent was all the more symbolic of sin. By paying attention to her, Jesus was increasing her shame. "O my God!" he cried silently.

"How long have you lived like this?" His voice was quiet, concerned.

"Eighteen years." Her voice was more quiet yet. She could have added, "two months and fifteen days." She remembered well the day of her paralysis and the slow bending of her spine. She came to synagogue regularly, despite the shame of it, to thank God that at least she could now walk.

"May I know your name?"

"Marise. May I know yours?" Although, she thought, we should not be speaking with each other—anywhere, anytime, let alone in this holy place during the service.

"Jesus, of Nazareth."

"Ahh. Friend of Martha. You are a healer."

"Yes." Jesus looked to the front of the synagogue where Lazarus had just rolled up the scroll and sat down. There was a meditative silence. Jesus set his jaw, moved quickly down the center aisle and stood directly in front of the scroll of the Torah. From that position, he called out:

"Woman, you are freed from your weakness, your disability!"

Heads whipped around to see who the stranger was addressing. She had followed him down the middle aisle, moving slowly and painfully through the women's section, then through the men's section. She was glad she couldn't see their faces now. There would be shock and probably outrage. Well, she would follow him.

She stood, still stooped, close to him. He laid his hands on her shoulders and she began ever so slowly to straighten up. Unused muscles screamed in pain, but she would, she would be healed. Suddenly standing tall, she began to praise God at the top of her voice. Allelu-YA! Praise YA!

The ruler of the synagogue was horrified, enraged. He began to shout at the congregation who had witnessed the healing and were buzzing with awe. "We have six days for working. Come on those days to be healed. Do not break the Sabbath, and never in my synagogue!"

Jesus turned toward him. "Sir, you have something to say to me?"

The president turned away, his face almost purple. Lazarus, right up front, was grinning at Jesus. Jesus wasn't smiling. He had something to say first.

"This woman who has been bent for all these years is precious in God's sight. What better work of God on any day, but especially on this holy day, than healing. Healing of her spine, yes, but healing of her heart. Healing of your hearts, too, you know. We must change our minds and hearts about who is sinful and who gets shunned. We oppress those already hurting. We point fingers and blaspheme our God, saying God must be punishing her. No, the Spirit of God has

151

anointed me to open the eyes of the blind, to straighten the backs that are bent, to proclaim God's favor. Praise our God!"

Jesus looked around the synagogue, meeting every eye, and then focused on the woman standing up front, next to him. Now he smiled—broadly. Taking her hand he led her down the aisle. Lazarus jumped to his feet and began a rousing hymn of praise. With laughter and clapping, the congregation joined in, while the leader of the synagogue tried to slip through the crowd.

### For Reflection and Prayer

*In our earlier prayer exercise with this woman, you were invited to identify with her. Perhaps you will again, but at a deeper level. Try walking bent over—whether just around your room, or perhaps for an hour. Hear Jesus' words to you, calling you by name. Act out the woman's movements, pray her alleluia. Tell Jesus how you feel.*

*Is there someone else with whom you identify? Mary of Bethany, eager to please? Strapping young Lazarus, known for his fine voice and contagious laughter? Maybe you are most comfortable hidden in the congregation, noticing the healing unfold. Noticing Jesus in action is indeed a form of contemplation.*

*Read the story from the Gospel (Luke 13:10-17) and watch Jesus. How do you feel as you let the Gospel come alive for you? Tell him.*

*What if you feel like the president of the synagogue? No problem. Jesus, as he so often does, will come looking for you. Maybe that night he'll invite you to the inn in Bethany for a glass of wine. Jesus understands you so well that he has incorporated your character into a few of his parables. Jesus doesn't reject the elder brother of the prodigal son; in his story, Jesus has the father tell his elder son: "All I have is yours." That father loves the elder son who has been slaving to be good. The parable about the vineyard workers chosen at the break of day—Jesus understands their grumbling when those who have only worked an hour get the same wage. Jesus knows how hard you have been striving, but wants to tell you how generous God is. "Come on, kick back, raise your glass, praise YA! You are loved!"*

**Feeling Shunned.** God loves those of great desire, both Scripture and the saints assure us. Depression strips us of desire. We are listless, not wanting much but sleep, or to be left alone.

### *For Reflection and Prayer*

*Picture the leper in Mark 1:40-45 as he drags himself from the wilderness to the side of the road where Jesus will pass. Listen to Jesus' passionate desire.*

*Picture yourself as that leper, feeling outcast, shunned, ugly, full of oozing sores. You tentatively approach Jesus, fearful of more rejection. You fall on your knees, saying in such a hesitant voice: "Jesus, if you want to, you can make me whole."*

*Jesus replies with passionate desire, "If I want to? Of course I want to. Be made whole!"*

*Let Jesus' deep desires for your wholeness and healing sink into your heart. Share your lack of desire or your confused desires with him. You can borrow some of his desire for your healing.*

*Jesus stretches out his hand to touch you. Let his hand rest on your head or your shoulder for as long as you are comfortable. Remember, your nervous system cannot distinguish whether you are really being touched or whether this is your imagination at work. Faith assures you that you are really being touched.*

**When Depression Feels Endless.** As if in parentheses, the evangelist Mark inserts a poignant scene into the account of Jairus' frantic search for help for his dying daughter. A woman, like so many women, ashamed of the infirmity of depression, the weakness and isolation that too often accompany it, surreptitiously touches Jesus' garment (Mark 5:25-34). Like many who suffer depression because their body chemistry has betrayed them, this woman with an issue of blood "suffered greatly at the hands of many doctors."

Who is she, so afflicted for twelve long years? What has her discouraging search for a doctor, a medicine, just some human contact meant for her? How has she suffered? How has her silent suffering affected those who have loved her these twelve years? How has she prayed in her desperation and her deadness?

Eli had loved her once. When Sarah's normal flow of blood suddenly continued for a month, he was truly concerned and willingly paid for a physician. Eli, of course, had to leave her alone in a special part of their rather ample home. She was unclean. Their small daughter could attend her, but Eli strictly forbade his two sons even to look at their mother. Eli patiently explained the laws of uncleanness to the boys. The nine-year-old understood perfectly, but four-year-old Caleb fidgeted and questioned and cried.

"Your Eema has been cut off from God, Caleb. The rabbis warn us to stay away or we may become unclean, even if we accidentally touch her or use a chair she sat on."

"I want to touch her. I want to hug her. It's no fair. Our sister gets to hug Eema."

"Your sister is a girl, so it doesn't matter if she becomes unclean, Caleb." It is unfair, Eli thought. I want to hug my beloved too.

Eli was frightened of uncleanness. Touching lepers, corpses or women with a flow of blood made the Jewish male unclean, a state of alienation from God, the rabbis taught. No problem avoiding lepers. He had willingly endured the purification rituals after he had buried his stillborn daughter last year. Someone had to prepare her tiny body and Sarah had been too exhausted and grieved. Sometimes one had to take chances with God.

Now, suddenly, after a few weeks, Sarah's hemorrhage stopped. She purified herself ritually and came to her family with arms open, crying for joy, hungry for their embrace. Then a few months later, she whispered to Eli, careful not to touch him: "The blood will not stop. I'll go now into seclusion. I'm sorry, my love, to leave you with the children and the work. Please tell the children I love them."

Sarah dropped her head and moved toward the taboo part of the house, isolated again. Twenty-four years old and she was cut off from God, her family, life. If only Eli were not so strict. Many husbands let their wives handle some chores and deal with the children during their monthly flow. Eli was rigidly religious, wealthy enough to have set aside a special room just for her "time." Their daughter, at seven, would be old enough to handle the household, Sarah thought bitterly. Poor child. "Oh no, Eema!" wailed Caleb, racing in from play just as his mother closed the door to her taboo room.

Sarah couldn't bear to answer him or she too would wail. She was frightened about this flow. Was she dying? The pain was like a whipping, a slashing deep inside her abdomen.

Seven years later she knew she was not dying. Eli had spent so much money on doctors. Although none could prescribe a cure, Sarah knew her disease and pain were not fatal—at least not physically.

Emotionally, she felt dead. She had been unable to attend when her eldest became a *bar mitzvah*. She missed her daughter's wedding. Next year Caleb would become a man and she had not seen him grow. He had been a faithful visitor, pulling his stool close to her door, telling her of all the daily events of home and school, the news of the neighborhood.

Eli came less frequently. The only eagerness in his step or voice was when he had found a new physician for her. Again and again they were both disappointed.

A few months before Caleb became a *bar mitzvah*, Eli quietly, sadly, approached her door. "My beloved," he said in such a flat tone that Sarah was alarmed.

"Yes, my love?"

"Caleb becomes a man soon."

"Yes?"

"I too am a man, with a man's needs. I am afraid we will never live again as man and wife."

"I fear that too, my love. I long for your kiss.... It will not happen, Eli."

"I know. So I have asked our daughter to take you into her home. Her husband is willing. Then I will divorce you and take a new wife." Eli suddenly sobbed.

"Ay—eee!" Sarah moaned. In her years of isolation, she had often imagined this worst outcome. Now it was happening. She was prepared. She cut short her wail. "Eli, the rabbis allow you four wives. Please don't cut me off."

"I know, I know. The disgrace of being divorced...and I know this is just your body betraying you, my beloved Sarah. Your spirit is so close to God, no matter what the rabbis think. But if I don't divorce you, will you go to live with our daughter so the new woman can have this home? I promise you, any new doctor, I'll pay. Any cure, I'll welcome you home at once. The new wife will have to understand that you are always my first love."

So Sarah had moved. To another secluded room. Now eight years cut off from people, from simple tasks, from religious and family and community celebrations; now nine years, now ten.

It was in the twelfth year of her hemorrhage when, heavily veiled, she made her way through the streets of Capernaum. She had gone to report to the latest physician that his herbal concoction had done no good. More discouragement, weakness, shame, fear. More slashing pain and constant fatigue. Her life had no meaning. Although her daughter was kind, she longed for Eli. Caleb visited her less frequently as he began to court a young woman. She would miss her "baby's" wedding too.

"O Lord," she prayed as she walked. Just that cry, the cry of the poor, was her only prayer, called out in her room, on the way to doctors or in the middle of the night. "Those who are crushed in spirit, God saves," she promised herself reciting the psalm "How can I trust that? *Eloi, Eloi, lema sabachthani?*" her heart cried, feeling so abandoned.

She suddenly swerved to avoid contact with a group coming her way. They chattered excitedly. "Come, Mother!" A young woman pulled at her arm. "Come with us to see Jesus."

"Thank you, no."

Now another group, a couple, then three young men, running and darting and calling, "Hurry! He's coming this way!"

She was heading into what was fast becoming a crowd. "Come on," another woman urged her, and then stood back.

"Sarah, how good to see you after all these years. Come with me, Sarah, to see Jesus."

"You know that I shouldn't even be on the street. And I am too tired. It's good to see you again, but I must get back to seclusion."

"Bah, Sarah! Those rabbis are to keep the men in line. We women are free from the Law. Of course, this Jesus says we're all free from these laws, a burden the rabbis put on our backs. And Sarah, Jesus heals! Amazing cures of the most awful diseases. Maybe he'll heal you. I'll ask him if I can get close enough."

"Yes, do. But I'll head home now, thank you."

Sarah dropped her head as she was accustomed and tried to avoid the crowd coming at her. "O Lord," she continued to pray. "O Lord, save me."

She suddenly stood straight at the thought. *Yesh* is the Hebrew word for "Yahweh saves" and Yeshua is Jesus' own name. "Shall I go to him?" The crowd determined her course.

"They are all unclean now," she thought as they jostled against her. "How will I know him?" she wondered.

She knew him. Just a few feet from a man whose eyes and entire body conveyed peace the crowd stopped. Jesus was walking purposefully next to the leader of the synagogue, and the people respectfully drew back as they passed.

Sarah came up behind Jesus in the crowd and thought, "If I touch even his garment, I shall be healed, saved."

Her hand inched out to his robe. Suddenly a power entered her body. Pain disappeared. Energy and then joy filled her entire self. "Alleluia!" she cried as loud as she could. No one heard for the noise of the crowd.

At that precise moment, Jesus stopped and wheeled around. "Who touched my garments?"

One of his disciples said to him, "You see this crowd pressing against you and yet you ask, 'Who touched me?'"

Jesus continued to search the faces in the crowd, his dark eyes piercing.

"I have made him unclean," Sarah groaned within. "O Lord, save me!" Fear subdued her new joy. She couldn't speak. Her body spoke for her. Trembling, she fell on her face before him.

He squatted next to her and touched her veiled head. "My friend," he said, "I felt power go out from me. Tell me, please, what has happened to you?"

Sarah lifted herself to her knees, and then took his hand as they both rose to stand face-to-face: the first man she had looked directly at in twelve years. "He is not supposed to speak to me in public," she worried. Wait—her religious worries and her shame were healed too!

"Allelu-YA," she said again, reverently.

"Yes, praise YA, our dear father God," Jesus echoed.

And then she told him the whole truth. The leader of the synagogue, agitated, tried to interrupt a couple of times, but Jesus ignored him. His entire focus was on this woman, one of the myriad who were crushed in spirit, now set free.

When Sarah had finished telling him of her physical pain and emotional isolation, how helpless, weak and alone she had felt, he placed his hands on her shoulders and looked, humbly and tenderly, into her eyes.

"Daughter, your faith has saved you and set you free. Go now in peace and be made whole."

"Thank you, sir."

Sarah turned and pushed through the crowd. Eli, Eli and my dear children! I am coming home!

### For Reflection and Prayer

*With whom do you identify in this story?*

*With Sarah? When have you felt crushed by depression, or slashed by any physical or emotional pain? Isolated? Abandoned by God? By your loved ones? Useless? Helpless? Go before Jesus now and reach out. See what happens when he turns to look at you.*

*With Eli? When has your rigidity and/or religious duty enslaved you? Cut you off from love? When have you watched helplessly as a loved one becomes more and more isolated? Go to Jesus. Ask him to come to your house to heal your dear one. If you are away from the one you love, "send" Jesus to your loved one. How does he respond to you? How do you feel?*

*With Caleb? When have you been separated from a parent? Felt bereft and abandoned? Could you, as that "lost child," climb on Jesus' lap and tell him how scared and lonely you feel? Could you let Jesus hug you right now?*

*Let one of our respondents conclude this prayer exercise with her response to Jesus:*

> You reach out to me and take my hand.
> You gently lift me from the ground,
> releasing my grasp from the hem of your cloak.
> "Shall we dance?" you ask.
> You are the tears in my eyes.

**Walking Away From a Toxic Situation.** Sometimes it is necessary for our health and well-being to walk away from harmful situations. Some people, places, events, situations can trigger depression in us. For example, sometimes we may butt our heads against a wall trying to make an impression, trying to fix a situation or even a person. We become more and more mired in the muddy swamp, a kind of quicksand effect. The more we struggle, the deeper we sink. This calls for "the wisdom to know the difference," as we pray in the Serenity Prayer, between what we can and cannot change.

Some conflicts simply cannot be negotiated. Then God's will for our peace calls us to walk away. Jesus himself gave us an example of walking away. His deep sigh was a bodily signal to him of the hopelessness of the situation:

> The Pharisees came forward and began to argue with him, seeking a sign from heaven to test him. He sighed from the depth of his spirit and said: "Why does this generation seek a sign? Amen, I say to you, no sign will be given to this generation." Then he left them, got into a boat again, and went off to the other shore *(Mark 8:11-13)*.

## For Reflection and Prayer

*Join Jesus in the boat. Let him tell you about his feelings and frustrations. How will you show him that you understand?*

*He asks you about what people or situations in your life drag you down. He listens to your stories and feelings without judging. He wants to help you sort out what is good and what is harmful for you. He wants to help you clarify your boundaries so that you can remain committed to realistic responsibilities and let go of toxic situations. Speak to him. Listen to him.*


**Receiving God's Tender Care.** Jesus told the story of a good Samaritan: "A man fell victim to robbers as he went down from Jerusalem to Jericho. They stripped and beat him and went off leaving him half dead..." (Luke 10:30-37).

A man, a woman, was traveling along an interstate highway. That man, that woman is you....

You fell into a dark place within yourself, a dark place where all your losses and burdens threatened to drown you in pain. Your sorrows stripped you, beat you, leaving you half dead. All the consolation of your religion, and even your spirituality, passed you by. When your friends saw you so sad and hopeless, they crossed to the other side of the road and passed by you.

But God, our tenting, traveling God, is coming near to you right now. When God sees you, God's compassion, God's suffering with you, rises up deep within God's heart. God stoops down to you and bandages your wounds, pouring oil and wine on them. Then, lifting you, God carries you to a place of rest and healing, a place of safety and peace, and cares for you.


## For Reflection and Prayer

*Rest for as long as you are comfortable in the realization that God cares for you right now, whether you remain aware of it or not. When you feel the pull of your depression, or when your worries about the ones you love return, replace your image with this image of God, the good Samaritan. You may do this for weeks or months before moving on to the next exercise. Please, take your time.*

## Oil and Wine

God, our good Samaritan, cleanses our wounds with wine and soothes them with oil. We can certainly carry that religious image and accompanying sensations and feelings with us. We realize, however, that God heals not only through direct religious experience, but most often through our human community.

Who in your current circle of loved ones is/are the wine and oil in your life? Mention each by name, being as specific as you can. Who in the past have been instruments of healing your heart-hurts? Again, mention them or write their names. If they have died, pause to remember them and thank them directly. If they are at some distance, think about writing to them. If they live with you or near you, thank them as soon as possible for letting God minister to you though them.

When Saint Paul encourages us to "Pray always" (1 Thessalonians 5:17), one way to do that is to say thanks to God or simply feel grateful whenever you remember one of these people. In more formal times of prayer, you can use this prayer of Paul's:

> I give thanks to my God at every remembrance of you, praying always with joy in my every prayer for all of you.... I am confident of this, that the one who began a good work in you will continue to complete it.... I hold you in my heart, you who are all partners with me in grace.... I long for all of you with the affection of Christ Jesus *(Philippians 1:3-4, 6, 7, 8, NAB).*

# The Grace of Coming Home

"Everything is grace!" These are the final words of the novel *The Diary of a Country Priest*. This masterpiece by Georges Bernanos is the fictionalized diary of a young French curate, an eloquent chronicle of trying to find meaning and light. The hero struggles with the bleakness of poverty and the grinding ordinariness of daily life. He is plagued by a chronic stomach ailment. He is depressed. Yet, in the end, he concludes that everything is grace.

This is our conclusion too. This chapter is grounded in the belief that everything is or can be grace in our wrestling with depression. In our struggle, we are finding a home within our self, accepting our one and only life with its limits, flaws, grace and growth. In this chapter, we will suggest ways we can cooperate with God's healing of the dis-ease of depression. We will also offer testimonies to some of the graces of depression itself. These are almost impossible to recognize when depression grips us by the throat, but we notice them in retrospect when the darkness has fled.

## Hidden Grace

One of the best short pieces on the topic of depression and spirituality is found in an article by Virginia Ann Froehle, R.S.M., entitled "Depression's Hidden Grace" (*St. Anthony Messenger*, January 1991). Some of our respondents have also written of the grace and gifts of depression. A woman writes:

> I know in hindsight that God was with me through
> years of depression, though it was not easy to discern
> God's presence. There are still some dips into

depression, although much more mild than before.
Now I see them as times of real intimacy when God
tells me more about myself or about God. Depression
seems to be an opportunity for revelation or
enlightenment.

A woman who struggles with chronic depression wrote out of
her paralysis and sense of guilt. The grace of her disease is a
new image, a new interaction, a deeper experience of God:

> Lord, what kind of God are you...?
> Who moistens clay with dryness and
>     lightens dark with deeper night?
> You fill my emptiness with empty space
>     and parch my throat with greater thirst.
> In new awareness of poverty and sin, I hear.
> You shout in silence
>     "I love you.
>         I love you."
> And in a hug which can't be felt
> You lift me up again
>     Abba—God
>         and whisper
>             "I am here."

Clearly God is present for her, even in what seems a tangible
absence.

Our personal experience of the heartbreak of depression
can attune us to the pain of others. So often in depression the
caring attention of another human being becomes the only
face of God. Louisa, on the threshold of forty, three years ago
began graduate school to study theology. She wrote to one of
her professors who, with Louisa's permission, passed it on to
us. This teacher of theology has had only three personal
conversations with Louisa over about three years. Aware of
how steady and supportive Louisa's husband has been
through the "fog," Mary is amazed at how a few hours of her
simple listening has been so important in Louisa's journey.
Louisa writes:

...I sit basking in the warmth of my woodstove.

Through the windows, fragments of pine branches and stark trunks, roots well buried, are all that is visible through the grey fog enveloping earth and sky. This landscape seems appropriate for a reflection on depression. The grey fog resembles that place in myself where joy and beauty are hidden under a cloak of darkness.

My visit with you was a chance to lift the fog and peer out another window. Though I feel like I'm dead and seek nothing, I realize that in seeking you I'm seeking God. If I'm seeking God I must be seeking life. It seems that I've crawled through a lifetime with despair and darkness crushing this flame called spirit. No burning sun to lift the fog inside and bring rich forests of color to life.

I think I have believed in the wrong God. I wonder what faith will do for me now. Have I always been abandoned? What is it like to be accompanied by God? What is it like really to be touched, really to feel?

This is hopeful: I have sought you like a lighthouse in the fog. I am no longer alone in this fog which separates me from grace. I can accept the emptiness, knowing that God is reflected through your face, Mary. It's a revelation that I can find God through other people. When we first met and I told you my story, you affirmed the grace in my life. I thought I knew God. I didn't realize that the real grace in my life was having you there to affirm grace. Blessed be this God I have yet to know!

God's compassion takes flesh not only in occasional intense encounters like Louisa's, but also in the daily, ordinary comforts of nature and the small kindnesses of friends, "the touch, literal and figurative, of my friends, family and colleagues," writes a man, a social worker with the homeless. He writes:

God is both present and absent for me in depression to the extent that I am connected or disconnected to other persons. God fills my eyes with real tears as I begin to come out of depression, realizing that, as I have depended, now others are depending on me to heal their broken hearts and bind up their wounds. That is God working in and through me.

One of our elderly respondents writes about waiting, watching amid the fluctuating emotions of depression, for touches of felt grace:

> I think there is a long period of time that passes before one senses that God is close to the brokenhearted. God is there, but closeness? No. That sounds contradictory, but we are so enmeshed in the confines of our humanity. That God does come close in time is the initiative that God takes, and then our openness and singlemindedness leads to closeness. This is not a be-all and end-all state; one is mindful of this almost every hour. It is a constant contact, an awareness that God is close. The closeness could be a beautiful blue sky, the kindness of a friend, a cheerful phone call.

## Call to Awareness

Depression can be a mid-life "wake-up call" that invites us finally to deal with old wounds, pain that binds us and keeps us from a grateful enjoyment of the ordinary. Depression, paradoxically, can be an invitation to accept the reality that "We are God's work of art" (Ephesians 2:10, *New Jerusalem Bible*). A prominent educator writes of her new awareness:

> At mid-life I came to the realization that I had been depressed for a large part of my life. Depression for me was a normal state. Yet I knew I was different from others. My life seemed to be meaningless. Years of depression had left me weak, hopeless and uncaring. The time had even come for me to consider ending this life. Then I heard a small, quiet, rational voice from my innermost being encouraging me to keep on living. After all, I was God's child and God was well pleased.

Even stronger than the most excruciating pain, the kind that often seduces to suicide, is the awareness that God's passion and ours are one. Pam, a competent nurse, is also involved in a variety of volunteer activities. She was, however, sexually abused as a child and is overwhelmed periodically by a depression that has led to suicide attempts. God is her savior:

> God feels my despair, my loneliness, my pain. God
> longs for my healing, for my living life to the fullest.
> It is easier not to fight, not to ask or to seek answers,
> easier not to change. Yet within me there is a power
> that will not let go, will not give up. Even if I choose
> not to live, God will not forsake me. My cries are
> God's cries, but a billionfold. My wounds are God's
> wounds, my broken heart is God's broken heart. God
> is more than close to the brokenhearted; God is the
> brokenhearted!

Joe, now a drug and alcohol counselor for young adults, has been through his own private hells. His way of making sense of the pain and depression in his life is to envision God as one who wrestles him to the earth and breaks his heart. The grace of depression is new strength:

> God breaks hearts to train us in the art of letting go,
> to toughen us against all we will have to leave on the
> day we die, to deepen us while we live.... God is like
> a strong wind. We are those spring seedlings blown
> flat. Without this wind our roots are shallow and our
> stems are thin and weak.

## Depth

Undoubtedly some people suffer and neither reflect on nor integrate the meaning of suffering in their lives. For those who dare to do so, a hidden grace of depression is depth. This usually is apparent only in retrospect, and often it is more evident to others than to ourselves.

Paul Tillich, a Protestant theologian, explains that it is in depth that we find God. God is the depth dimension of all reality. Tillich named God the ground of our being. To touch depth in human events and especially in human persons is to touch God.

Half a century earlier, Gerard Manley Hopkins knew God as the ground of all being. He reflected on the terrible loss of life in his poem "The Wreck of the Deutschland," a ship that foundered in the mouth of the Thames. Hopkins noted that God was "past all grasp," truly a mystery. Yet God, he asserted, is "the ground of our being and granite of it." As a prayerful Jesuit, burdened with deep depression, still he searched for God in all things. In another of his poems, he acknowledged God as the "dearest deep down freshness" of all things. Could God be the dearest deep down freshness even in our pain, suffering and confusion?

In our culture we spend much money, time and energy on entertainment, "dancing as fast as we can." We are perhaps too aglow with glitter, until the Challenger explosion or the bombing in Oklahoma City galvanizes the nation and challenges us to reflect. To those whose depths have been carved and hollowed out through suffering, each new pain of others provides a new capacity for feeling with, for compassion. At the same time, paradoxically, trust deepens, trust that "all will be well, all manner of thing will be well," as medieval woman mystic Julian of Norwich proclaimed.

Sean Sammon is often asked what he learned through his suffering stemming from the tumor on his pituitary, from those symptoms that felt like depression. He responds:

> Illness leaves you between lives, the one you knew and another that awaits you. Then, you were in control, enjoyed the upper hand; now, the future is less certain, beyond your power to shape.... 'So what have you learned?' people ask. That's just the point—midlife illness doesn't teach you anything. Instead, it helps you understand, for the first time. And you know full well that understanding will someday answer to the name of wisdom.

## Seasons

Many poets, artists and ordinary folks have compared depression to the winter of the spirit. As the changes of the seasons and the earth's struggles to be fruitful offer us symbols, so one of our respondents, a middle-aged married woman, can now be grateful for the seasons of her life. Although her relationship with God, imaged as the rugged north face of a mountainside, is far from comfortable, she finds consolation in her gardening.

> I find the divine when I am gardening. It is healing to touch the seasons, the cycle which leaves space and time for the depressive, for the sadness and loneliness that form a part of every life. The north face of God is simply one aspect of life in the garden. It has its season.

## Hope

One of the hidden graces of depression is God's gift of hope. It seems that hope is forged and strengthened in pain, even hopelessness, and yet hope is a force for healing as well.

Saint Augustine once wrote that hope has two daughters: anger and courage. Hope also includes a new creative and creating vision of reality. Without its daughter anger, hope can be a Pollyanna-ish, sugar-coated wishing. Anger, even outrage, over situations of injustice, whether personal abuse or cultural violence, fuels the hope for a better, more communal life with peace and justice for all. Courage, hope's other daughter, is needed to change what we can. Without courage to act, anger can so easily find its outlet in violence against the self or others. Anger and courage coupled with vision leads to and continues energizing the gift of hope we received in baptism.

The vision of hope springs from imagination. Imagination plays with possibilities, and play saves us from the deadly seriousness of fanatic vision. Father William Lynch warns us in *Images of Hope* about absolutizing, especially absolutizing our righteousness, our personal understanding of justice. Too easily, he writes, we substitute law for grace, which cripples our imagination and can lead to mental illness. In theological terms, absolutizing is our making of idols. Our absolutizing instinct lives and thrives in darkness.

Vision, on the other hand, plays in light, creating, discarding, re-creating, changing, letting go, trying something different. This kind of creative imagination, instead of puffing us up in perfectionism, actually gentles our tendency to grandiosity. This kind of imagination is not product-oriented; we need not produce artistic masterpieces. This kind of imagination is of the earth, the dirt, which in Latin is *humus*. Born of the earth (*humus*), rooted in our bodies as an internal sense, imagination grounds (*humus*) us in that basic reality: we are creatures and God is God. To know that fundamental reality in our whole self and to live from that reality is humility (*humus*), leading to a deeper reverence for humanity (*humus*): our own, Jesus' and others'.

Humility and humor, also offspring of hope, temper the anger and courage of which Augustine writes. Anger is loaded with power, a force that springs from and energizes our whole self, motivating and moving us. Anger signals that we have been violated, at least as we perceive it. If our vision is true, some of our angers that might spring from a sense of entitlement will shrivel. If our vision is flooded with light, our perspective is clear and we can laugh at our punctured pride. Blind rage, animal violence, revengeful fury can gradually give way to more truly human anger. Our anger, more clear and more direct, can be put at the service of ourselves and society.

The other daughter of hope, courage, also calls for humility and humor. The perspective of humor helps us discern when courage is prudent—actually the Spirit's gift of fortitude— and when it springs from unreflective impulses. Humility defuses what could seem grandiose when we have to take courageous stands, as for example Martin Luther did when he proclaimed: "Here I stand. I can do no other." Courage, psychiatrist Rollo May argues in *Courage to Create*, undergirds creative responses. Creativity is foundational to hope.

God calls us to hope in prayer, especially in our prayers of intercession. Research indicates that imaging good health can heal disease; imaging restful scenes can relax our muscles and slow our heartbeat. We need to image—picture, hear, feel, smell, taste—scenes of justice and peace, healing and hope. When we pray for the needs of the world, we need to image them as graphically as possible.

We, with God's own longing, passionately long for people to feed each other, listen to each other, honor each other. Ignatius of Loyola, Teresa of Avila and Therese of Lisieux tell us that God appreciates this prayer of great desire, vision and hope.

## Becoming God's Compassion

We offer one final biblical image for depression: exile. Exile is certainly not a simple journey, replete with plans, maps and adventure. Nor is it, at least initially, a pilgrimage. On the contrary, it often feels quite disconnected from the holy, from the goal of God. Exile happens to us, often by surprise. We are carried off to unfamiliar lands by hostile forces. Our new identity is refugee, migrant, displaced person. We long for home, and we are captive. Feeling desolate, we turn in hope to God's promise:

> Our God is bringing back the exiles,
> Healing the brokenhearted,
> Binding up their wounds (see *Psalm 147:2-3).*

According to Matthew's Gospel Jesus, Mary and Joseph experienced that forced migration, a terror that drove them to an alien land where they became refugees. They went to Egypt, the land of ancient slavery for their people. The truth for our salvation is that from his infancy Jesus knew exile.

> My dwelling, like a shepherd's tent,
>     is struck down and borne away from me;
> You have folded up my life,
>     like a weaver who severs the last thread....

> Like a swallow I utter shrill cries;
> I moan like a dove. *(Isaiah 38:12, 14)*

Our God is a tenting God, writes Jeremiah. The Word became flesh and pitched his tent among us, writes John. Foxes have dens, birds have nests and Jesus has nowhere to lay his head. At times on the mountain Jesus must have cried, and we cry: "O God, you have always been our home!" (see Psalm 90:1).

God cries to us: My dear one, *you* have always been my home! Our tenting God, in exile, makes a home with us, inviting us to put flesh on God's compassion. Even in our dis-ease, we are chosen. God wants us as we are so that once again, even in our weakness, God's compassion may be embodied. In our weakness the power of God may grow strong.

As our respondent Pam summed up, "becoming God's compassion" is a deep union with God:

> My cries are God's cries, but a billionfold.
> My wounds are God's wounds. My broken heart
> is God's broken heart. God is more than close
> to the brokenhearted. God is the brokenhearted.

This kind of "passion-with" is not virtue that we practice. We do not volunteer for this kind of union. "It was not you who chose me, but I who chose you and appointed you to go and bear fruit that will remain," Jesus assures us all (John 15:16).

We can gradually uncover many hidden graces in the midst of and after depression. The greatest of these graces is love. Love means "bearing one another's burdens" as Paul would phrase it (Galatians 6:2). "From [Christ's] fullness we have all received, grace upon grace upon grace," is how John's Gospel proclaims the union (John 1:16). Jesus, according to Luke's Gospel, invites us to "Be compassionate just as your heavenly Father is compassionate" (Luke 6:36, *New Jerusalem Bible*). This is profound union with God.

One of our respondents, a woman in her early seventies, has been forged in wisdom through enormous losses. She has lived through the death of her first husband, her five-year-old daughter, her teen-aged son. More recently, the sudden death of her twenty-eight-year-old son was followed, just nine months later, by that of her thirty-one-year-old daughter. She resonates deeply with her bereft grandchildren and has changed her life to rear one of them. This woman—warm, passionate in her feelings and caring—has become God's compassion in the flesh for her family and friends.

Compassion has a number of components. We begin with the body, its passions and desires, its memory and imagination. From personal compassion, entering into the world of another, we attend to the possibility of entering—with God—into the world of all others.

Our bodies, our first sources of knowing and understanding, must enter "into" the passion and suffering of the other. This "bodily thinking"—or perhaps we would say knowing—is how Luke would describe Jesus' compassion. The evangelist Luke chooses a Greek word we could translate as "bowels" or "gut": "his gut was moved with compassion," to show how Jesus' whole body was wrenched in feeling with others.

Empathy involves our entering into the world of another. This is precisely what God wanted to do—and did do—in the Incarnation. In a bodily, enfleshed way, God entered into our emotional life and our suffering.

To enter into another's world calls for memory and imagination. Often in this book we have referred to Jesus as our pioneer. He blazed the way. As such, in his risen body, which is still a human body, his memory and nerve cells are imprinted with the events of his life, as well as the feelings and desires with which he lived those events. As our pioneer, he can remember and continue to enter into every human emotion with us. He has felt every one, and he remembers.

As Jesus, so us: Our bodies, our memories of each human emotion, help us, too, to become God's compassion. We are an incarnation in today's world of God's love in action. As Pope Pius XII affirmed in his encyclical *Mystici Corporis*, on the Body of Christ, we the Church "are Jesus Christ, extended in space and time and communicated to humankind."

Our imagination is central to empathy. Some may wonder at this point: "I've never had much imagination. How is this possible?" Imagination here is not a matter of artistic or creative ability. To enter the world of another, which many of us do quite well each time we listen carefully, is an act of imagination.

To enter in and be with another is probably the greatest gift one human being can offer another. It is a call, an invitation, a gift from God, but one, like faith and hope, that flooded us at Baptism. It is the gift of love.

Love is always in process. We never finish. Not only a baptismal gift, love is also a fruit of the Holy Spirit (see Galatians 5:22). If love is fruit, we might liken depression, then, to the manure that every fruit tree needs. Depression can help love grow.

Since depression is so common a human condition, it impresses on us that we are like all other human beings. That is the beginning of healing our inordinate craving to be special. We learn that we are in no position to cast a stone at anyone. As we learn to accept that others are flawed, we learn to accept that so are we. Even the authorities in our lives and others whom we may have idolized are merely human. "[God] knows how we are formed;/remembers that we are dust" (Psalm 103:14).

After acceptance, in this lifelong process of learning to love well, God may offer us the gift of forgiveness: of self, others and God. Forgiving is not an act of the will, however. We may try to make it one, but ancient hurt and current resentment will leak out in strange ways. Certainly depression is one expression. "Forgiveness is God's gift," asserts John Patton, pastoral counselor and author of *Is Human Forgiveness Possible? A Pastoral Care Perspective* (Abingdon, 1985). Forgiveness is grace, never our achievement. To rush forgiveness is harmful to everyone's health.

From her praying with the passion narratives, one respondent noted that even Jesus on the cross did not say: "I forgive you." Perhaps it was too soon yet for him to have worked through this crushing rejection by his own compatriots, God's own people. So he prays for the gift of forgiveness, crying out: "Father, forgive them." As Jesus, so us.

Mary stood at the foot of the cross as truth for our salvation, surely pondering forgiveness in her heart. Yet it may have taken years. Eventually, as Rose Kennedy said about her life of sorrow and the faith that sustained her: "After a storm, the birds sing."

Mystery, according to Jesuit theologian Karl Rahner, is that which is infinitely knowable. Compassion, like all mystery, is infinitely knowable. It begins with the gift of being able to enter the world of one other, but gradually we are gifted with the desire and ability to enter the world of all others. This calls for the moral courage of which May writes in *The Courage to Create*: "...moral courage springs from solidarity in suffering which begins with seeing the suffering, pain and evil." Courage is "the capacity to move ahead in spite of despair" at the heart of us. In reality God is at the heart of our beings, deepening and widening our capacity for compassion. Because God is at the heart, there is room in our hearts for everybody.

Everybody is welcome to call God "home." In this place of exile, as we slowly become God's own compassion made visible and tangible in this world, social conditions, poverty, homelessness, economic injustice, violence may cause depression. It is possible, writes Scripture scholar Walter Wink, that this kind of depression is healthy. When we stand against the powers of evil, when we envision the pain of the world, when we feel deeply in compassion with the violated and war torn, depression can be normal and healthy, he writes.

Emotions are signals. Sadness, grief and even flatness or absence of emotion may be a signal. The kind of depression about which Dr. Wink writes may be a signal that we have been yoked in bearing the burdens of God. The friends of God feel with God. Prophets are so close to the mind and heart of God that they dare to speak in God's name. More, they feel God's own passion for justice, for peace, for love.

Listen to the prophet Jeremiah:

> My grief is incurable,
>     my heart within me is faint....
> I am broken by the ruin of the daughter of my people.
>     I am disconsolate; horror has seized me.
> (Jeremiah 8:18, 21)

Grief on behalf of others gripped Jesus too. Jesus not only had compassion for the crowds. He felt deeply with his God. Imagine Jesus reading the scroll of Jeremiah, letting these words of God's own grief sink into him as rain and snow penetrate the earth. Jesus wants to make the tears of God fruitful. How can such grief be fruitful?

Whenever we share God's grief, we let God deepen our compassion with others. Paradoxically, this kind of union with God's own heart is exquisitely joyful and peaceful as well.

God's plans and passionate desire for our peace surely motivated Jesus' mission to the lost and outcast of Israel. His hearing God's cries in the poor, the abandoned, the outcast, pained him deeply and created within his own heart the good news that he would preach to the people. For centuries God had wept over Jerusalem. Jesus' own tears were the tears of God made visible, audible, tangible. "If only you knew the things that make for your shalom!" is Jesus' cry to his people, and to us.

Jesus' mission flows from his union with God, the God who wants our peace. Jesus will take up our burdens so as to share life with the God who bears burdens. That union energizes him for his healing mission of proclaiming the *good* news. He himself offers to catch the tears of God. And he will wipe away our every tear.

### For Reflection and Prayer

*Find a piece of colored paper, preferably green or blue; construction paper would be ideal. Cut out six, seven or even more tear-shaped drops. On each drop write one of your sorrows.*

*Try to feel your sadness as you write. Don't hesitate to cry. When you have finished, gather your tears and hold them, palms upward, in offering to Jesus. Look at him looking at you, tenderly, and with infinite sadness in his eyes. Let him speak to you. Wait. Listen.*

Union with God is like a dance. God shares the pain of the world with us; we share the pain of our own life with God. God offers us compassion, a home for our heart in the land of exile.

> You found us in a desert land, in the howling waste of the wilderness. You encircled us and cared for us, guarding us as the apple of your eye. Like an eagle that stirs up its young, so you spread your wings to catch us and bear us up. You lifted us up on eagle's wings. No strange god, but you, you alone are our leader (*Deuteronomy 32:11-12*).

We offer God a home in our hearts, healed and healing. Nothing is lost, not one tear, not one sigh. All of it has been forming us to become God-with-flesh-on. When dark days return, we will be able to dip deeply, immersed again in God's continuing compassion. In swamp and in exile, in peace and in light, wherever we find ourselves, we are coming home. We are slowly and surely becoming God's compassion.

> God is close to the brokenhearted. Those who are crushed in spirit, God saves.

# BIBLIOGRAPHY

Becker, Ernest. *The Denial of Death*. New York: Free Press, 1973.

Berg, Richard, C.S.C., and Christine McCartney. *Depression and the Integrated Life*. New York: Alba House, 1981.

Bernanos, Georges. *The Diary of a Country Priest*, trans. Pamela Morris. New York: Doubleday Image, 1937.

Billig, Nathan. *To Be Old and Sad: Understanding Depression in the Elderly*. Lexington, Mass.: Lexington Books, 1987.

Burns, David. *The Feeling Good Handbook: Using the New Mood Therapy in Everyday Life*. New York: William Morrow, 1989.

_____. *Feeling Good: The New Mood Therapy*. New York: William Morrow, 1980.

Callahan, Rachel, C.S.C., and Rea McDonnell, S.S.N.D. *Hope for Healing: Good News for Adult Children of Alcoholics*. Mahwah, N.J.: Paulist Press, 1987.

_____. *Wholing the Heart: Good News for Those Who Grew Up in Troubled Families*. Mahwah, N.J.: Paulist Press, 1991.

Copeland, Mary Ellen. *The Depression Workbook: A Guide for Living With Depression and Manic Depression*. Oakland, Ca.: New Harbinger Publications, 1992.

Cronkite, Kathy. *On the Edge of Darkness*. New York: Doubleday, 1994.

Duke, Horace O. *Where Is God When Bad Things Happen?* St. Meinrad, Ind.: Abbey Press, 1991.

Froehle, Virginia Ann, R.S.M. "Depression's Hidden Grace." *St. Anthony Messenger*, January 1991, pp. 10-17.

Harrington, Wilfrid, O.P. *The Tears of God*. Collegeville, Minn.: The Liturgical Press, 1992.

Heckler, Richard. *Waking Up Alive: The Descent, the Suicide Attempt, and the Return to Life*. New York: Putnam, 1994.

Hopkins, Gerard Manley, S.J. *The Poems of Gerard Manley Hopkins*, fourth edition, eds. W. H. Gardner and N. H. MacKenzie. London: Oxford University Press, 1967.

Kazantzakis, Nikos. *Zorba the Greek*. New York: Simon & Schuster, 1953.

Kesey, Ken. *One Flew Over the Cuckoo's Nest*. New York: Viking, 1973.

Kübler-Ross, Elisabeth. *On Death and Dying*. New York: Macmillan, 1970.

Lewis, C. S. *A Grief Observed*. San Francisco: Harper & Row, 1989.

Lindemann, Erich. "Symptomatology and Management of Acute Grief" in *Crisis Intervention: Selected Readings*, H. Parad, ed., New York: Family Services Association of America, 1967, pp. 7-21.

Linn, Matthew, S.J., Sheila Fabricant Linn and Dennis Linn. *Good Goats: Healing Our Images of God*. Mahwah, N.J.: Paulist Press, 1992.

_____. *Healing Spiritual Abuse and Religious Addiction*. Mahwah, N.J.: Paulist Press, 1994.

Lynch, William F., S.J. *Images of Hope: Imagination as Healer of the Hopeless*. Baltimore: Helicon Press, 1965.

Manning, Martha. *Undercurrents: A Therapist's Reckoning With Depression*. San Francisco: Harper, 1994.

May, Rollo. *The Courage to Create*. New York: Norton, 1975.

McDermott, Brian O., S.J. *What Are They Saying About the Grace of Christ?* Mahwah, N.J.: Paulist, 1984.

McDonnell, Rea, S.S.N.D. *When God Comes Close*. Boston: Daughters of St. Paul, 1994.

Miller, Alice. *For Your Own Good: Hidden Cruelty in Child-Rearing and the Roots of Violence*. New York: Farrar, Straus, Giroux, 1983.

Parkes, Colin. *Bereavement: Studies of Grief in Adult Life*. New York: International Universities Press, 1972.

Phillips, J. B. *Your God Is Too Small*. New York: Macmillan, 1961.

Puls, Joan. *A Spirituality of Compassion*. Mystic, Conn.: Twenty-Third Publications, 1988.

Raub, John Jacob. *Who Told You That You Were Naked? Freedom from Judgment, Guilt, and Fear of Punishment*. New York: Crossroad, 1992.

Redmont, Jane. "Praying in a Time of Depression." *America*, August 26, 1995, pp. 14-20.

Robbenolt, Roger. *Tales of Gletha, the Goat Lady*. Easton, Kan.: Forest of Peace Press, 1991.

Sammon, Sean. "Midlife Tumor." *Review for Religious*, March-April 1995, pp. 276-278.

Satir, Virginia. *Peoplemaking*. Palo Alto, Calif.: Science and Behavior Books, Inc., 1972.

Styron, William. *Darkness Visible: A Memoir of Madness*. New York: Random House, 1990.

Valentine, Mary Hester, S.S.N.D. *Aging in the Lord*. Mahwah, N.J.: Paulist Press, 1994.

Viorst, Judith. *Necessary Losses: The Loves, Illusions, Dependencies and Impossible Expectations That We All Have to Give Up in Order to Grow*. New York: Simon and Schuster, 1986.

Wink, Walter. "God Is the Intercessor." *Sojourners*, November

1990, pp. 23-24.

Wolff, Pierre, S.J. *May I Hate God?* Mahwah, N.J.: Paulist Press, 1979.